INTO *the* HIGH COUNTRY

JASON CRUISE & JIMMY SITES

Into the High Country: Spiritual Outdoor Adventures
Copyright © 2006 by Jason Cruise and Jimmy Sites
All rights reserved

ISBN 10: 0-8054-4180-8
ISBN 13: 978-0-8054-4180-2

Broadman & Holman Publishers
Nashville, Tennessee
www.broadmanholman.com

Dewey Decimal Classification: 242.642
Men / Devotional Literature / Outdoor Life

Printed in Belgium
2 3 4 09 08 07 06

CONTENTS

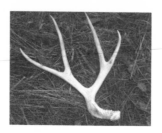

ABOUT THE AUTHORS

Jason Cruise is the founder of Outdoor Ministry Network, a nationally recognized ministry effort designed to help churches establish outreach to hunters. He has pastored churches in Texas and Tennessee and speaks across the nation to outdoorsmen. He is the author of *The Heart of the Sportsman,* as well as executive editor of *The Sportsman's Bible.* He lives in Franklin, Tennessee, with his wife, Michelle, and their son, Cole—who's just itching to get in camo and out in the hunt.

Jimmy Sites is the host of *Spiritual Outdoor Adventures,* a television show seen weekly in 30 million homes, as well as a Tuesday morning radio show on the Salem Network. He is a widely sought speaker and teacher, a husband and father, and co-pastor of New River Fellowship—a man driven by twin passions: the call of the wild and the call of the Lord. Jimmy, Amanda, and their two children, Christin and Jonathan, live in an Old Timer Log Home in the hills north of Nashville.

POSTED: NO TRESPASSING TILL YOU READ THIS!

There's more than one way to hunt. You know that. There's the spot and stalk, stand hunting, ground blinds, drives. You can hunt from a drop camp, you can hunt while sleeping in the comforts of a cabin and return each day, or you can slip out from work and just go for a few hours.

And just as there are all kinds of trails that take you to the hunt, there are all kinds of trails that can take you into this study.

YOU CAN HUNT ALONE

Sometimes it's what you prefer. You just need to get out there and settle your soul, go at your own pace. In the same way, you can travel the trail of this book individually, all by yourself, creating time just for you and the Lord.

YOU CAN HUNT WITH A BUDDY

We've all got our favorite huntin' buddy. He's got all the dirt on us. He knows all the dumb things we've done or said over the years while in the field. He vividly remembers all the times when we've missed . . . and the times we haven't.

So, if you want, use this study as a time of spiritual growth between brothers. Create your own trail. Choose to go into the high country once a week, or every few weeks. The thing is, you need to meet together to talk over your hunts.

You need to compare notes. Discuss what you've seen and felt. We promise you this: you'll get out of it what you put into it.

YOU CAN HUNT FROM CAMP

Setting up camp takes a little more effort. You have to do some prep work on the front end, but man! Are great memories forever created! Some of our favorite stories have roots that go back to hunting camp.

If that's more your style, use this as a small group Bible study. In fact, that's one of the foundational reasons we chose to write it.

When it comes to providing real ministry to outdoorsmen, you must have a way to plant roots that bring them back for matters of the heart. Churches today are lacking any real material that can help disciple an outdoorsman. We hope this book will fill that void and make spiritual growth challenging and rewarding.

Try a weekly meeting. Have each person come to the group ready to discuss the chapter assignment. As a leader, you must do the prep work to keep the discussion moving.

Or meet twice a month. This allows time to let things settle in the heart. It takes a little longer to get through it, but that's fine if you want to plant roots.

Just do it your way. Create your own plan. Let the group decide the route they want to take . . . *Into the High Country!*

PRE-SEASON

*Happy is the man who finds wisdom and
who acquires understanding.*

Proverbs 3:13

*It's been a long time coming. You bought a few
extra arrows that you probably didn't have to get,
but it just felt right. You're not quite sure if you want
to stay with a 150 grain bullet or move to the 180.
You've been checking out that new spotting scope.
Or a range finder that'll come in handy. Wool parka
or Gore-Tex? The questions continue. You go to your
gear closet more often now, and that only makes
it worse. Now it's just a matter of survival—
surviving the wait until opening day.*

OUTFITTED *for* LIFE

Gear . . . just the sound of the word does something to you. Real outdoorsmen can never really have enough of it.

I love getting new gear for my outdoor pursuits. Love it! More than Sun Drop bottled in the can, more than chocolate cake, maybe even more than ribs from my favorite barbeque haunt. When UPS pulls up at the office to drop off my most recent Cabela's order, I literally cannot wait for the guy to get in the door!

As for my family, what do they buy me for Christmas? Yep, you got it. More gear. I do believe from my own stash I could probably outfit most of my neighborhood for a day trip in the field or on the stream.

If you love the outdoors, I'm sure you can relate. (I'm sure your wife can relate, too— *painfully perhaps.*)

But the problem with a gear obsession is that it won't make you a better hunter or angler. It'll make you a little more prepared, maybe, but it won't make you better at cornering your quarry in a wild pursuit.

To be quite honest, a lot of today's gear is faddish and often unnecessary. You know it as well as I do. One of my friends in the outdoor industry, a famous TV personality (whom I'll leave nameless), said it best, "Most turkey calls are made to call the hunter, not the turkey, just as many fishing lures are made to catch the angler."

MOST TURKEY CALLS ARE MADE TO CALL THE HUNTER, NOT THE TURKEY, JUST AS MANY FISHING LURES ARE MADE TO CATCH THE ANGLER.

FISHIN' OR CATCHIN'?

I saw this truth unfold before my very eyes as a kid. My dad was absolutely phenomenal when it came to smallmouth bass. He wasn't on TV, and he's never written a book about smallmouth strategy. But I've been a personal witness to countless endeavors on the water as I watched him drag in those fit-throwin' smallmouth. (*I'm not ashamed to say that if a smallmouth were a man, I wouldn't want to fight him!*)

When going for smallmouth, my dad would hover close to only a handful of lures—the chosen few. Sometimes it was a beat-up, paint-chipped crank bait. Or just a purple and red spinner bait. Or a few others in between.

As for me? I was loaded down with gear, even

at the age of ten! A bloated green Plano tackle box was my beacon to the world, exposing my own personal lure display. Some kids collected baseball cards; I collected Rebel Wee-R. And of course, Rapalas. And spinner baits. And plastic worms. And God only knows what else.

See, my dad owned a small outdoors store, and I was his best customer. (Well, not exactly. I was really his best *welfare* case, sporting a bunch of new gear he'd had to ante up for!) But Dad was the one who caught the fish.

Why?

Because Dad *knew* smallmouth bass. He knew their habits, their personalities, their tendencies, their hangouts, their deepest desires. It wasn't about his gear; it was about his knowledge. I learned from watching Dad that there is *fishin'* and then there is *catchin' fish!*

MORE OR LESS?

Now that I'm older, I see the same trends in hunters, especially turkey hunters. A person new to turkey hunting will spend 90 percent of his time learning to cluck, cackle, fly down cackle, fly up cackle, yelp, assembly yelp, purr, purr and cluck combo, cutt, and even learn how to imitate a fight.

I'm absolutely convinced, however, that if a new turkey hunter would spend 75 percent of his time actually getting inside the mind and heart of a turkey, and 25 percent of his time learning how to sound like one, he'd fill his tag every spring.

In other words, there are guys who hunt for

turkeys, and then there are turkey hunters.

The bottom line: Know your animal. Know why they do what they do. Learn what makes them gravitate to certain environments and what works in a given situation. You've got to ask the deeper questions to find the real answers.

THE BOTTOM LINE: KNOW YOUR ANIMAL.

And gear won't do that for you.

Yet we remain obsessed over getting new stuff for ourselves. Famed financial guru Dave Ramsey calls it "stuff-itis." That's because wanting more is what's killing Americans today. The quest for more leaves you a shallow person. You end up a mile wide and an inch deep.

REFLECT

1. *How much money do you spend on gear each year?* $ _____*

   * This is one of those times you may need to go ahead and secure a hiding spot for this journal—just in case your wife runs across it!

2. *How much of what you buy, in percentages, do you think you actually need?* _____%

LOOK AT THE BOOK

When I considered all that I had accomplished
and what I had labored to achieve, I found everything
to be futile and a pursuit of the wind.
—Ecclesiastes 2:11

The richest guy who ever walked the earth was a man named Solomon. You can read about him in Ecclesiastes, one of the books he wrote, where he recorded what he had learned from all his pursuits for significance and meaning in life.

More than just money, Solomon had acquired both money and power—and an endless supply of both! If he didn't have something, it was only because he didn't want it.

If you'll go ahead and read the whole second chapter of Ecclesiastes, you'll see how Solomon went out on this experiment to buy, sell, build, acquire, and possess everything he could. Kind of hard to wrap your mind around that kind of financial freedom, isn't it?

Imagine saying to yourself, "I will deny my heart no pleasure," which is sort of the gist of chapter 2, verse 1. "I'll go buy new vehicles to help accommodate my mood for any given day. A Ferrari for days when I need speed, a Chevy 3500 HD for days when I need towing power, a Caterpillar for days when I just feel the need to move stuff around, a convertible Bentley for days when I need to impress someone, and a Hummer for days when I just need a testosterone boost."

And that was just for starters for a guy like Solomon. Yet this guy came to the end of his experiment and basically said, "You know, it was fun, but I still don't feel complete inside."

Isn't that the way it always is? Once you sift through all your stuff, you find that your relationship with God is the only thing that can really satisfy the soul. Fads and new glittering gadgets are never a sure bet.

DIG DEEPER

So you and I are forced to ask life's tougher questions. We must not avoid them. The hardest questions to ask are the one's aimed at the man in the mirror.

• *How deep is my heart?* Am I avoiding real life lessons and real truth in my pursuit to get more?

• *Can I be content?* Am I able to take what God has given me and use it to the fullest? Or am I always delaying success because I want the next thing?

• *Do I really know who I am?*

These are the questions that matter. And how do you dig down to find the answers?

First, you must be willing to go there. You cannot be afraid of the soul shovel.

Second, you must be willing to deal with what you find. What's the point if you won't let it change you? Are you willing to dig? Solomon was.

FIELD JOURNAL

Name 2 things that you want most right now:

1.

2.

Why do you think you want them so badly?

Are you trying to use them to fill a deeper void?
Is this desire to possess things masking deeper needs?

FROM THE HEART

Jesus had the amazing ability to teach complex truths in simple terms. The first time Jesus ever preached a sermon, he had a lot to say about life. And when he came to the issue of what you desire most, he said:

"For where your treasure is, there your heart will be also" (Matt. 6:21).

Stop just for a second and read that short section from the Bible—Matthew 6:19–24. How have the truth of Jesus' statements borne themselves out in your life?

POSTSCRIPT

All outdoorsmen see gear as an investment. And it is. You invest in it because the end result means something to you.

But rods break. Tree stands become outdated. Scopes lose their optical power. These are all earthly goods made with the intention of lasting less than a lifetime.

What kind of investments are you making in eternal things?

EXPLORING NEW
TERRITORY

The Cessna 206 cruised at an altitude of 200 feet above the Alaskan tundra. Grizzly Adams was flying it . . . or at least a guy who looked like Grizzly Adams. My good friend Mike McCrary of Alaska Bush Sports was captain of the cockpit. With long flowing red hair and a ZZ Top beard to match, Mike could easily pass for a Viking warrior. Instead he is one of Alaska's best bush pilots, and he is at the top of the list for getting adventurers into places where no plane has landed before. He is also an incredible man of God.

I had come to Alaska in pursuit of a fly-fishing adventure. With cameraman Brandon Chesbro in tow, along with friends Luc McKinney and Terry "Nutt" Chesnut, my goal was to document some incredible stream fishing, while also securing some close-up bear footage of coastal browns.

Alaska is the land of a million streams. You can literally look in any direction and see water. So how does one know where to start?

It's simple . . . scout.

Fly low and cover lots of territory. Look for clear water. Watch for bears along the streams feeding on salmon. Check the waterfalls for migrating fish that are trying to jump to the top. Get close enough to see fish swirling in the pools below.

It's an awe-inspiring thing to witness snow-covered mountains looming far above your plane window, and yet see a paint factory explosion of color in the wild flowers below. It's even more awe-inspiring when next to those flowers you see a school of torpedo shaped salmon shooting through a shoal in a creek the width of a two-lane road.

These are the things we spotted as we covered over a hundred miles of Alaskan wilderness.

GRIN AND BEAR IT

After landing at a spot that was forgiving to the nose gear of the 206 and setting up camp along Contact Creek, we commenced to catch more fish than I ever imagined a White River fly rod from Bass Pro Shop could handle. We caught grayling, Dolly Vardin, arctic char, rainbow trout, and king salmon. The size range was 2–40 pounds!

The bear wish came true as well. We saw six different coastal browns, including one that snuck in on me while I knelt down near the creek, filming a gear scene for Brunton's Optimus NOVA multi-fuel stove. We had to wade the creek to get away from that one! The next day a sow and cub worked their way along the opposite side of the stream from us, and a huge ten-foot male gorged himself on blueberries on the hillside, often rolling on his back just to bask in the sun.

The final bear encounter was when a juvenile boar decided he wasn't supposed to be scared of us and came roaming right into camp. The over-the-shoulder footage of this bear is incredible, as I held my rifle at the ready while the bear sniffed my backpack twenty yards away and opened his jaw wide enough to bite a basketball. He finally left us alone. We filmed all of these bear encounters and came home with an incredible story for a *Spiritual Outdoor Adventures* episode.

All of this happened because we took the time to explore new territory rather than going back to the same old familiar spot that gets fished year after year.

> **WE TOOK THE TIME TO EXPLORE NEW TERRITORY RATHER THAN GOING BACK TO THE SAME OLD FAMILIAR SPOT.**

SAME OLD SAME OLD

This is an important concept for outdoorsmen to realize, no matter how experienced we are.

For three decades I have been a member of the Prospect Hunting Club in Warren, Arkansas. We have thirty members and four thousand acres. Sixty-six elevated box stands are spread out along power lines, gas lines, and old roadbeds throughout the property, and bucks have been harvested from every stand. Yet I still find myself returning year after year to the same old ones: Joe Bond #5; North Pipeline #2; REA #7; Cedar Tree Stand; South Power Line #2. Lemonade Stand.

Maybe this is because I'm so sentimental. I remember every deer I've seen from these stands. Every buck that has dropped in my crosshairs. The muzzleloader kills. The first deer taken by my wife and son. The snapshots captured by my daughter. The eight-point my dad shot while I videoed.

It's almost as if I'm investing my minutes like dollars in the low-risk mutual funds of deer hunting that these proven stands provide. All the while, though, there may be a higher-risk, more aggressive fund out there just a mile away that offers much bigger dividends (like 130-class bucks or better).

Or maybe there's an entirely different motivation at work here. It could be that I'm just overly superstitious about such matters.

When I played college baseball for Harding University, I wouldn't wash my socks if I was the winning pitcher. During my senior year when we won the championship, I remember pitching a five-game stretch without a loss. My socks were so dirty that when I took them off, they would stand on their own in the corner of my dorm room! I did everything exactly the same during that stretch of victories. My routine was predictable because of my superstition.

Last year, however, I decided to buck tradition

(no pun intended) and try something different at the Prospect Hunting Club. Rather than returning day after day to the same old familiar territory I had hunted for years, I decided to expand my horizon and go to an area I had never hunted before.

Three hundred acres of woods had been clear cut, and a block of several hundred acres of dense pine thickets bordered it. An old abandoned railroad track ran through these dense pine woods about a hundred yards from the clear cut. I could see a couple of hundred yards down the old railroad bed, but realized that I wouldn't have much time to make the shot if a buck crossed.

I decided to give it a try anyway.

OTHER SIDE OF THE TRACKS

With two hours of daylight left, I settled in with my gun resting in the half-ready position. Only fifteen minutes had passed when a doe came running across the railroad bed with a buck in hot pursuit. He crossed so quickly that I didn't even have time to get my gun up. The buck was a decent six or eight-point with an average rack, similar to the deer I was used to shooting from my traditional stands.

In the next few minutes, the doe circled in my direction and actually led the buck to within fifteen feet in the thicket behind me. I couldn't see them because the brush was so thick, but I could certainly hear her heavy breathing and his hot grunts. She then retraced her tracks back to the railroad bed, but she never crossed. This scene repeated itself two more times.

Then something amazing happened.

As the doe finished her third circle away from me toward the old railroad bed, this time she decided to go on across about 150 yards away. I quickly put my gun to my shoulder, anticipating the average buck to follow. What stepped out, however, was not average—at least not at our hunting club in south Arkansas!

A long-bodied, wide-racked, tall-tined, thick-massed bruiser of a buck in full rut stepped out into the railroad bed with his tongue hanging almost to the ground. I didn't even have to think twice. I found him in the crosshairs and barely had time to squeeze off a shot before he disappeared into the dense pine thicket.

That couple of seconds was all I'd needed. He piled up only five feet from the railroad bed, his twenty-one inch inside spread making him look all the bigger when I walked up on him and saw those horns jutting up from the ground.

This incredible new memory, this set of horns on my wall that I will see for the rest of my life, never would have happened had I not chosen to explore some new territory. I guess you could say I got out of my rut and enjoyed an entirely different rut – that of a big ol' buck that was inhabiting the new place on my expanding horizon.

IN THE RUT

I think there's an analogy here for our day-to-day lives.

As humans we are so prone to get in ruts. This applies to parenting, marriage, work, personal habits, and the list goes on and on. A rut is nothing more than a grave with no end. Ruts can kill us spiritually, or at least make us so dull that we're barely getting our bat on the ball when we could be slamming home runs for God.

Answer these questions:

Are you satisfied with the way you're raising your children? Are you happy with the way your marriage is going? Are you pleased with your spiritual walk with God? Are things going well for you at work?

If your answer is no to any of these questions, think about this: if you keep doing things the same old way, you will keep getting the same old results.

Maybe it's time for you to explore some new territory. Scout hard. Expand your horizon. Read some books on parenting. Attend a marriage seminar with your spouse. Start reading your Bible on a daily basis, and make a commitment to start attending classes at a local church. Serve some people at your work rather than only being served by them. Replace that bad habit with a new good habit. Change stand locations. Do things differently.

Get out of the rut before you get so bogged down in it that you'll eventually die there.

HIGHER GROUND

Ironically, when you begin to explore new territory and do things differently, it's like starting out on a fresh adventure. Compare it to scouting a new piece of property that you're going to be hunting this fall or spring.

You enter for the first time and work your way through the perimeter to the core of the property. You look for ancestral deer trails or heavily used roosting trees. You look for scat on the ground or tracks in the dirt. You search out food sources, watering holes, and sanctuary thickets. You find the persimmon candy store and the clover restaurant. You carefully check out the old rusty fences for the crossing spots, looking for white belly hair hung in the barbs.

Finally you feel informed enough to make a major decision—where to hang the stand or set up the blind. You're proud of your efforts.

You walk away excited, refreshed, anticipating a great season in the near future. The possibility exists that you've even learned something new about a sport you've loved for years.

Do you get excited when you think about exploring new territory? I certainly do. And for me, it's even *more* exciting when I explore new *spiritual* territory. Walking new ground or flying over new terrain is always exhilarating, but it's especially so when I'm exploring that ground with God—the very One who created it! I love going deeper in relationship with God, allowing Him to take me to a level I've never been before.

He is an incredible Guide. He knows the terrain of my life like no other. He has things in store for me that I cannot begin to fathom in my small brain. All I have to do is set out on the adventure of claiming these blessings and trust that He will be with me always. I know He will.

The same is true for you.

REFLECT

1. *Ruts are nothing more than graves without ends. What ruts are you in right now in your daily life? (List at least two.)*

LOOK AT THE BOOK

The Old Testament book of Numbers, chapters 13–14, contains a story about twelve men who were chosen to do some dangerous scouting. They were appointed by the national leader, Moses, to spy out the land of Canaan on the west side of the Jordan River. This is the land God had promised to give to the Israelites. They were given a specific mission:

> *"Go up this way to the Negev,*
> *then go up into the hill country."*
> *—Numbers 13:17*

The twelve spies explored for forty days, then they returned to Moses and the Israelites, bringing with them some fruit and some stories from the land. They reported that the land was everything God had promised it would be, but that there were large fortified cities with giants living in them.

At this point in the story, ten of the twelve spies made a huge mistake. They discouraged the Israelites from attempting to move in and conquer the land of Canaan. They reported that the people were too powerful and numerous. "We can't go up against those people, because they are stronger than we are!" (Numbers 13:31).

When the other two spies strongly disagreed and tried to convince the people that the land *could* be conquered with God's help, the ten skeptical spies began to spread rumors among the people that the land wasn't really fit to live in. They stirred up the people to the point of almost having Moses, his brother Aaron, and the two courageous spies killed.

DIG DEEPER

Here's an exercise for you. List the names of the ten skeptical spies who were afraid to conquer the new territory:

1	6
2	7
3	8
4	9
5	10

My guess is you didn't write a single name in one of those blanks. However, you probably *can* name the two courageous spies who wanted to conquer the new territory. (If you don't know the answer, you can find a complete list of all twelve spies in Numbers 13.)

1	2

The point is simple. A person who's scared to conquer new territory in life positively impacts no one. Only two adventurers in this story were walking with full faith and trust in God as their Guide. And they ended up being the only ones allowed to enter the promised land of Canaan when Israel took possession. One of them even became the leader of the nation.

FROM THE HEART

Check all the following that apply to you at this point in your life:

❏ I am ready to explore some new territory with God as my Guide.

❏ I want the unclaimed victories that God has already promised He will give me.

❏ I am ready to experience a deeper relationship with God and give Him more of myself than I ever have before.

❏ I hunger for the blessings that come from walking with God on a daily basis.

❏ I am not afraid of the unknown because God is with me everywhere I go.

❏ I want to just keep doing things the same way I've been doing them, and keep getting the same results I've been getting.

POSTSCRIPT

Remember, you are never alone when you walk with God. Trusting in Him as your Guide makes all the difference!

"For He Himself has said, 'I will never leave you or forsake you'" (Heb. 13:5).

Therefore, you never have to fear the unknown, because God is with you wherever you go. Ready to explore some new territory?

IN *the* BEGINNING

I t seems to me that the single most stable thing we can count on in life is change. As odd as it may sound, the fact that things never stay the same is one of the few things you can actually count on. Life seems to be all about new beginnings.

Being a follower of Christ is no different. It involves the constant reshaping of your life to meet His. So if you can't handle change, you'll have a hard time with life on the God trail.

Keep in mind, though, that change is difficult if you think of it in terms of loss, in terms of what you're having to give up. Yet it's amazingly welcome when you think of it as a new opportunity.

Have you ever noticed how many times in the Scriptures when God touched someone's life and changed it, He even changed their name? Names carry our identity, and God changes our identity when we come into Christ.

Jesus offers that second chance for us, the chance for a new beginning, the extra arrow in the quiver when you thought you were out of options, the chance to trod ground never before seen.

For hunters, new beginnings are monumental experiences. They are memories deeply etched into the fabric of our souls. Probably because they only happen once.

FIRST SHOT

Take your first gun for instance. For me, it was a .410 single shot that my dad bought for me. Dad usually accompanied me on most of my outdoor endeavors, but being a small business owner, he simply couldn't get out of work the day I took this gun out into the field for the first time. So my granddad took me to shoot it.

My grandfather goes by the name "Dat." I ascribed this glorious title upon him when I was just a minnow, most likely because I couldn't get out the word "granddad" just right. "Dat" seemed good enough, and it stuck. Sticks even to this day.

We hopped in his truck, accompanied by a longtime pal of his named Dunn. He was the sort of fella you'd want around when you were going to shoot your gun for the first time. He just kinda fit the mood.

I never remember seeing Dunn without a large stack of tobacco in his jaw. His words echoed with an accent and inflection that can only be accomplished through the perfect, Deep South recipe of life. He was a good friend.

I rode in the middle, feet straddling the hump on the floor, the CB radio right in front of me as we journeyed out to a remote area around Estill Springs, Tennessee, to shoot this new cannon of mine. I remember the first shell I loaded into the breech. The hull was green with a shiny brass cap. Dat showed me how to load it. Dunn added his encouragement by saying, "Don't be afraid of it, boy! Pull that trigger!"

The hammer fell. *Boom!* A new beginning.

FIRST KILL

What about your first deer? For me it was a half-racked three-pointer. One of my dad's employees had taken me on a midday hunt to do a slow spot and stalk around my favorite farm. We hadn't been there ten minutes when we jumped this bedded buck. He was a monster to me! I remember throwing up my old Marlin 30-30 and watching him run away through the scope. Then, as if on cue, he stopped and looked back. The sun was behind him and in front of me. His big bodied silhouette illuminated radiantly as I stared at him through the crosshairs. I couldn't believe it.

Finally . . . a chance at a *buck!*

My ten-year-old frame shook from the adrenaline. I fought the battle of ten men as I tried to keep that gun steady. *Was he going to run? Could I get the shot off? Don't miss!* All these thoughts flashed in the frame of two seconds. Finally I felt as if I had it steady enough.

The hammer fell. *Boom!* Crash of a downed deer. A new beginning.

REFLECT

*Describe your favorite "new beginning" in the outdoors.
(If you're using this book in a group, tell us all about it.
Don't leave out anything!)*

LOOK AT THE BOOK

*In the beginning God created the
heavens and the earth.—Genesis 1:1*

*In the beginning was the Word . . .
and the Word was God.—John 1:1*

As you may know, the word *genesis* basically means "new beginning," the origin of something new. Long ago I understood that the heavens and the earth began with God. That made sense and Scripture confirmed it. It was the ultimate new beginning.

Yet I've forever been intrigued by John's Gospel. I love his book for many reasons, but mostly because of how John so uniquely introduces his Gospel account. He didn't launch into the narrative like the other writers did. He began by just telling us, "In the beginning . . ."

Sure, the Old Testament starts out as a new beginning, but so does John's Gospel. While the heavens and earth were a new beginning, so was the coming of the Word (a metaphor for Jesus Christ.)

Jesus brought a new beginning!

God is forever creating new beginnings for us. It starts with our birth. We're thrust into this "enemy occupied territory," as C. S. Lewis calls it. We grow up and receive the wounds life gives. We realize we need a Savior. Then we discover that there actually is one! And He creates for us a new beginning, launched by His forgiveness, followed and upheld by His strength every day.

DIG DEEPER

The great thing about opening day of a new hunting season is that it holds brand new promises. What kind of animal will fill your tag? How big will he be? Will it happen fast, or will it be a slow stalk? Each season creates new memories.

Each season offers a fresh start.

Life isn't all about hunting, though. (You and I forget that sometimes.) So where in your life do you need a fresh start? A new beginning? Where could you most use a new season?

Lost the connection with your son? You can get it back if you want it.

Lost the vibe between you and your wife? You can start again.

Where do you need a new beginning? Why?

_____

_____

_____

_____

_____

_____

_____

_____

_____

_____

_____

_____

FROM THE HEART

If there is an area where you need a new beginning, then you're faced with a choice. And the choice is: *Now what? What will you do about it?*

If you know you need to reconnect with your son or daughter, now what?

If you need to make amends with a hunting buddy, now what?

Jesus Christ gives us new beginnings, but we have to accept them. We have to move in and embrace the offer.

Write a prayer, telling God where you need a new beginning . . . and what you're willing to do about it:

POSTSCRIPT

God is the author of opportunity. If you feel like you've stepped on His last nerve and can never find peace again, try asking Him. Try trusting Him. Try letting Him decide what's just around the corner in your life.

EARLY SEASON

From the creation of the world His invisible attributes, that is, His eternal power and divine nature, have been clearly seen, being understood through what He has made. As a result, people are without excuse.

Romans 1:20

Finally. You're back in the hunt. There's a smell that comes with it that's hard to describe but still undeniable. A mixture of fresh earth, hardwoods, sage, and (best of all) the uncluttered air. Open space. It's the anticipation of what might happen this season.

SANCTUARY

The buck sported 10 gnarly points. Deep brown. The color of an acorn. Twenty inches wide. G-2s a foot long. Thick neck. A brute in any hunter's category.

He was the dream buck I had hoped to see, and I was looking at him from twenty-five yards.

The giant white oak tree was like an oversized cereal box, pouring out its contents each morning, ringing a dinner bell with each gust of wind as the acorns showered the ground. And that's where the buck was feeding, deep in the shade of that mighty oak.

Two years earlier I had decided to quit bush-hogging a twenty-acre area around this spot, allowing the food plots to grow up. The grass and weeds reached waist high the first year. By the second year they rose to my shoulders. As this new season began during the third year, the growth was dense with briars and vines.

A month before the season I had hiked in to check out the area. "Perfect," I thought to myself, scouting from a distance with my Brunton Epoch binoculars. "This is going to hold some good deer, especially when hunting pressure is applied on neighboring farms."

Developing sanctuary is a great tactic for drawing deer. Whether it's pushing down a few trees and leaving the tops, allowing a field to grow up, planting a pine thicket—or all of the above—when you develop sanctuary, you create a safe haven for wildlife.

PURSUING SAFETY

Just think for a moment what it would be like if you were a deer. Every second of every day, you're watching your back. You're constantly the prey, ever cautious, wary of predators, always hunted. That's why deer love sanctuary. It offers safety, which provides them with peace and relaxation.

In a sense, the same can be said of humans. During the three years I lived in a cabin in the Ozark Mountains of Arkansas, I had a sanctuary of my own. I called it my *hermitage*—a place especially set aside for silence and solitude.

My hermitage was a small one-room cabin sitting on the edge of a slope of woods. I had a large window installed so that I could look out through the trees and watch the wild animals. This cabin hermitage became a mental incubator for me.

It was there that I spent time reading God's Word.

It was there that I responded to God in prayer—verbally, silently, and through journaling.

It was there that I would sometimes express my thoughts through quiet song.

And it was there that I sat in silence . . . meditating . . . reflecting . . . listening with inner ears for God's impressions upon my heart. The cabin hermitage was an important place for my spiritual life.

In ancient Russia, every village had its hermitage. They called it a *poustinia*. In our society today, we have no such religious sanctuary within our communities. That's why it is so important that each person individually seek out a hermitage.

It may be in your own home. A room set aside for prayer and Bible study. A room supplied with religious books, Bibles, journals, and perhaps a CD player for listening to soothing recordings and religious songs.

The hermitage may be something as simple as a well-worn recliner or a dinner table. It could be an attic room or, as in my case, the back porch of my Old Timer Log Home lodge sitting on the edge of the hollow. It could be almost any quiet place in your home which, when being used as a hermitage, remains off limits to the rest of the family.

SEEKING QUIET

All hospitals have hermitages. They're usually called chapels or prayer rooms. Even large businesses are beginning to see the need for such a place. Many executives are setting aside a "Quiet Room" for their employees to use during their breaks or lunch hour, to give them a place to unwind and relax.

A church building is also a wonderful place for a hermitage. A small room set apart for silence and solitude, for quiet prayer and Bible study, will serve as a blessing to many who need a place to get away from people for a while. Some, because of their family situation, find it impossible to have a hermitage at home. They just need a place where they can come and quietly approach God with no distractions from others.

It doesn't really matter where your hermitage is. What matters is that you have one. You need to spend time in solitude and silence. You need to spend time daily reading the Bible, praying to God, reflecting, meditating, and discerning His will for your life.

God is waiting for you. Will you meet Him?

By the way, if you're wondering what happened to that big 10-point, he didn't even give me time to draw my Mathews Solocam bow. The wind swirled, blowing my scent in his direction for just a millisecond. Needless to say, he was gone just as quickly as the gust of wind.

You don't have to guess which direction he ran. Within a few bounds he was back in his own hermitage, back in the sanctuary where he would hide for the next four years. I should know. Because this year, I harvested him.

REFLECT

This chapter emphasized the importance of developing sanctuary for wildlife. Imagine that you were put in charge of developing a 100-acre tract for hunting. Where would you place your sanctuary and how would you develop it? (Draw an aerial map below, designing the tract according to how you would want it to be.)

N

W   E

S

LOOK AT THE BOOK

*They are to make a sanctuary for Me so that
I may dwell among them.—Exodus 25:8*

God made this interesting statement about
"sanctuary" to Moses, the leader of the Israelite
nation. So it was God Himself who came up with
the idea for sanctuary. What need did He see in
us that caused Him to do that?

_____

_____

_____

DIG DEEPER

The sanctuary created for God by the Israelites
was called the *tabernacle*. The sacred ark of the
covenant was kept there in the Holy of Holies.
Only the high priest could enter the Holy of
Holies into God's presence on behalf of the people,
and even he could enter only once a year. Later
the tabernacle (a temporary tent) was replaced
by the temple. But the Holy of Holies remained
intact, along with the ark and the regulations the
priests were to follow.

Moving forward a few centuries, a follower of
Jesus named Paul was inspired by God to write
in 1 Corinthians 6:19–20: *"Do you not know that
your body is a sanctuary of the Holy Spirit who
is in you, whom you have from God? You are not
your own, for you were bought at a price; therefore glorify God in your body."*

FROM THE HEART

How do we keep ourselves—our bodies, our hearts, our minds—a quiet, peaceful place for the Holy Spirit to dwell in?

_____

_____

_____

When Jesus died on the cross, His blood purchased you from the captivity of sin. At the same moment, the heavy veil separating the Holy of Holies from the remainder of the temple was torn in two from top to bottom. This symbolized that God was moving His dwelling place to another temple—the human heart—just as Paul said.

So when you accept Jesus Christ as your Lord and Savior and claim His blood in full obedience to His will, your heart becomes the temple—the tabernacle—the sanctuary of God! He is not only *your* sanctuary; you are His!

Think of a place that could be your sanctuary, where you could spend private time with God.

POSTSCRIPT

Just like that ten-point buck, you can escape the spiritual death of sin by fleeing for sanctuary to the outstretched arms of Jesus. Just follow the blood trail!

A FIXED POINT

To say that my first trip into the high country was memorable would be an injustice to the experience. To call it "memorable" would be so generic . . . like saying that the Sistine Chapel was "pretty." It's just not right to put it that way!

Believe it or not, I learned a lot on this hunt. Hunts have that ability. Every hunt can be a teaching moment sent from God Himself, if we'll let it be. My third and last day chasing northwestern muleys was most certainly a day where God showed me something I needed to know.

But before we take a step forward, I must take you a few steps back, in order to give you some perspective of what I was dealing with.

I grew up in Tennessee. And other than my years of study, I've lived my whole life there. So I don't have any trouble knowing where I am on a hunt in the hilly countrysides of the South. Land navigation has never been a problem for me.

My wife, Michelle, on the other hand, gets turned around at Wal-Mart! Seriously. Her complete inability to remember where she is has been the source of many, many laughs for both of us. Maybe that's why God led her to me. I am her personal GPS—and I don't even require batteries! Michelle helps me be the kind of *man* God wants in the home, and I help her *find* the way home. It's all about teamwork!

Yet my sense of land navigation was put to the ultimate test when I hit the high country of Oregon.

ROCK IN THE WILDERNESS

Everything looked the same to me there. I mean, in the South you've got ridges, creek bottoms, valleys ("hollers," as we call them.) You have fields to guide you, and most of the time you've got roadbeds to use as landmarks. On top of that, you've got a buffet of various trees. Hickories, pines, white oaks, beeches, poplars, cedars, just to name a few.

On this ranch out West, however, all I had was land. Lots and lots and lots of land. And juniper trees. Everywhere I looked there were juniper trees.

Now I'm sure that to the locals, there were lots of variations in the land. Even I could see that there was some contour about me. Rim rock, creeks, that kind of stuff. Yet for the most part, it all looked the same. I had to learn quickly to find a fixed point to keep me on track.

So I chose the largest one I could find—Mt. Hood! Call me simplistic, but I figured something as large as Mt. Hood, miles upon miles in the background, could always be seen.

The third morning felt promising. Fairly soon out of the gate I was on a few muleys.

Does.

That was fine, though. I reasoned that an interested fella overcooked on testosterone couldn't be too far away!

I was using a hunting method I was familiar with—ridge hopping. I'd done it many times before, especially on farms where I could get longer lines of sight. I'd glass ridges and sit for long periods of time. And it was working.

Yet on this particular morning, each time I went down into a canyon, I would come out on top at a different point than when I started. I'd go down expecting to come up at the same point on the other side of the next ridge, but I'd always be about 150 yards off, one way or the other.

No big deal, it's just that I'd have to walk all that extra distance to stay on the line of travel I needed to be on.

So again, I decided to use my fixed point methodology. Looking around, I had one option. A lone tree. Yep, you guessed it. A juniper. Three canyons away, sitting atop the ridgeline, stood my lonely friend. All by himself. It was perfect. I'd line up with him,

YOU'VE GOT TO THINK LONG-TERM WHEN YOU'RE COVERING A LOT OF GROUND.

walk straight into the mouth of the canyon, and each time I'd come out exactly in line with him. It kept me from turning a four-mile walk into a six-mile trek!

You've got to think long-term when you're covering a lot of ground. You need to reserve as much energy as you can, *when* you can. A fixed point was all I needed to maintain my energy supply, and boy, I'd need it at the end of the day when there was more hunting to do.

REFLECT

We're going to be talking about something in this chapter we're all craving for: rest. And in order to give it to us, God has instituted a rhythm into our lives that begins and ends with the Sabbath. It's a "fixed point" in our lives to slow down, step back, and cool our jets.

What have you gained the most from keeping the Sabbath? And what have you lost by ignoring it?

LOOK AT THE BOOK

Remember to dedicate the Sabbath day:
You are to labor six days and do all your work, but
the seventh day is a Sabbath to the Lord your God....
Therefore the Lord blessed the Sabbath day
and declared it holy.—Exodus 20:8–11

Sabbath. I'm afraid most Christians run right past it. Literally.

In today's church world, evangelicals are on the forefront of moral values. We're quick to scream at gambling, to combat pornography, to steer people away from drugs and alcohol, to hold high the call to personal integrity. All of these are noble and righteous pursuits..

We also do all we can to proclaim the need to show the Ten Commandments in public places. Yet I wonder if we actually try to remember them ourselves, to place them in our own homes and our own hearts.

Especially this fourth commandment.

Yes, we're willing to fight all the right fights. We'll even go on *Larry King Live* to prove it. Over the last several years our major battles have centered around family values. We believe in preserving those, and we should.

Yet I wonder if the church can be just as guilty of aiding and abetting the decline of the family when it comes to this one specific issue: spending time together.

Follow me for a second. Here's the lineup of the week for most of today's evangelical churches:

Monday: committee meetings, deacons meeting, aerobics classes

Tuesday: visitation and outreach

Wednesday: supper, kids activities, prayer and devotional times

Saturday: fellowship events of all sorts

Sunday: Sunday School, followed by morning worship, followed by Bible study again in the evening, followed by evening worship

A question to pastors: Have you ever wondered why only 5 percent of your congregation shows up at Sunday night worship? Three words—*they are exhausted!*

It's not always a lack of commitment! Instead of some corny slogan or cliché on the church marquee, I'm convinced that most churches should post: *We are burned out, stressed out, sung out, and give out . . . but the lights never GO out here at First Church of the Overcommitted.*

The itinerary I just listed is no exaggeration. In fact, it may be too conservative. But I'm a pastor, and I believe it's high time we gave our people permission to live a normal life!!

How can a dad be expected to be a real dad when he's made to feel guilty because he stayed at home one Sunday night to throw baseball with his son?

We're always hammering our people to win people to Christ. But the last time I checked, the best way to expose nonbelievers to the gospel is to actually spend time with them. Winning their trust. Gaining real friendship. Yet I wonder: if I'm supposed to take my nonbelieving buddy hunting in order to gain that trust, how can a guy do that when his church looks down on him for not being at the hot dog roast where the crowd consists of 100 percent Christians?

DIG DEEPER

There are a lot of ways you could reorder your life when it comes to Sabbath.

Maybe you need to tell your pastor, "I'm through serving on five different committees." Maybe you're a pastor, and you need to make the executive decision to cull some weekly events at your church.

Maybe you need to start coming home before 7:00 each night from work. Maybe the reason you haven't led any nonbelievers to Christ in the last decade is because you actually don't know any.

You need Sabbath . . . and you know it.

It's a commandment . . . and you know it.

This may be the most important question you've asked yourself in the last fourteen years. Where in your life do you need to be faithful to the Lord of the Sabbath?

FROM THE HEART

Reports and people polls have been telling us for years now that many Americans secretly feel lonely. They feel the need for more meaningful relationships in their lives. Yet the one thing we won't take time for is people!

Why are we working so hard to get so much, realizing the whole time that nothing earthly will go with us into eternity?

I believe God gave us the Sabbath as a fixed point. It was intended to keep us on track. It was given to us so that each and every week we could go down into the canyon of a busy world, yet come up to the top still on track because we'd readjusted ourselves with a God-designed navigational system.

Sabbath was given to us to keep our minds clear, our hearts untangled, our spirits fresh, our families intact, our lives in order. It allows us to do something we were commanded to do—rest!

As a devoted believer, you would shudder at the idea of breaking God's heart by willfully committing adultery, number seven of the commandments. You wouldn't dream of murdering a person and thus breaking the sixth commandment. So why do we scorn God's commandment of Sabbath?

POSTSCRIPT

Could it be that we aren't taking God's Sabbath commandment seriously enough?

THE NIGHT BEFORE

couldn't sleep. My twelve-year-old brain was traveling at warp speed as I laid in bed and created deer hunting scenarios in my head:

Would I get my first shot at a whitetail deer in the morning as my dad and I hunted together? Would it be a close-up, standing-still shot, or a long-range walking shot? Would I drop the deer in its tracks or end up having to track it? Would I really have to drink a cup of the deer's blood or take a bite of the heart (as I had heard) in order to be initiated into the worldwide deer hunter's club?

These and a hundred other scenes played across the movie screen of my pre-teen mind. When I finally drifted off to sleep, it was restless at best. And when the alarm clock sprang to life, so did I. My dad certainly didn't have to drag me out of bed on the morning of my first deer harvest at the Elms Plantation Deer Camp near Altheimer, Arkansas.

Now, fast-forward thirty-one years, and change the location to the hill country of Texas. It was the final day of an October bow hunt, and I had passed several nice bucks ranging from 130 to 145 Pope and Young points. I had "set my sights" on a bruiser buck that would break the 160 barrier, a buck I had already seen roaming the Diamond C Ranch. I had caught a glimpse of him the first day in the field, but he had patterned me within four hours of my presence in his domain.

He was a smart one, but I was determined to outsmart him. We were deep in the chess game.

DEER IN THE HALF-LIGHT

On the final afternoon of the trip, my cameraman Don Belles and I decided to make a bold move. We ate an early lunch and headed out to a new area of the ranch on the backside of the hill where we had been hunting. We traveled about a mile away from where we had first spotted the tall-tined buck, found a sendero containing lots of deer sign near some thick woods, and poured out a couple of containers of C'Mere Deer powder on the ground. Then we climbed into an old live oak tree for the long haul.

Our theory was that the old buck had probably removed himself from whatever had violated his domain on the front side of the ranch and was now hanging out in the thickets on the backside, near the wad of does that were leaving tracks and droppings all over the sendero.

Our bold move began to pay off. About an hour before dark, the does and yearlings began easing out of the thickets and grazing. A small six-point buck discovered the C'Mere Deer powder and basically threw all caution to the wind as he buried his lips into the delicacy. He ended up fighting with a dominant doe (and losing) over his booth in the restaurant. Then, as if someone flipped a switch, the herd of a dozen deer became very nervous. I sat more attentively on the edge of my seat in the tree, following the gaze of the dominant doe, checking the edge of the thickets on the surrounding hillside.

That's when I saw him!

He had stepped out behind two other bucks and was looking in the direction of the herd of does below me. My brain accused my eyes of lying, but my eyes continued to yell to my mind that this was the biggest buck I had ever seen on the hoof. The rack on top of his head looked like a rocking chair as the buck began to saunter in my direction. His G-2s and G-3s had to be fourteen inches long. I was looking at the buck of a lifetime!

YES AND NO

Since the age of twelve when I first harvested a whitetail deer and was infected with the obsession of deer hunting, I have spent countless hours in the woods hunting in many different states for whitetails. I've probably killed over 100 bucks, but not like the one that was now twenty yards away, with my twenty-yard pin resting on his chest through my peep sight.

He was quite skittish and I knew he wasn't going to hang around very long. So I didn't waste any time as he took a step forward with his right leg, opening up the boiler room as an invitation to my Readhead Carbon Max 3000 arrow, tipped with a 100-grain, three-blade, "Bad to the Bone" Muzzy broadhead, propelled by a Mathews LX bow.

Pass-throughs are sweet and I've witnessed several, but this one was the sweetest of the sweet. The arrow entered and exited before the buck even realized he'd been stung. When the realization set in, he kicked and ran like a cat caught in a hornet swarm. He disappeared at full throttle into the thicket about ninety yards away. I was breathing so heavy I began to see black dots!

THE ARROW ENTERED AND EXITED BEFORE THE BUCK EVEN REALIZED HE'D BEEN STUNG.

The orange ball of the sun dipped below the Texas horizon as I climbed down out of the live oak tree. The air was already getting cooler, and I knew I didn't have much time to find the buck before pitch-black set in. Don lowered the camera to me by rope and climbed down. We decided to look at the footage to see exactly where the arrow had penetrated. We wanted to make sure it was a lethal shot before we went barging into the old buck's sanctuary, possibly jumping him from his bed and causing him to run before expiring.

(I've seen both does and bucks that were mortally wounded run a mile, leaving hardly any trace of blood to follow. I sure didn't want to take such a chance with this buck of a lifetime.)

After looking at the footage, it appeared that I might have hit the buck too far back to pierce the vitals. Don and I agreed that we should leave the buck alone for the night and come back at first light in the morning.

So we headed back to the camp house and began one of the longest nights of my life.

TOSS AND TURN

To say that sleep came sparingly is the understatement of the century. Once again I was experiencing the "night before" syndrome. The movie projector cranked up as always and began playing various scenes in my mind:

• *Big boy has already gone to deer heaven and is lying out there just waiting on me to walk up and count the points . . .*

• *He isn't fatally wounded and has already traveled a half mile away without leaving more than a few specks of blood . . .*

• *He's bedded down with a fatal but slow working wound, and as long as he isn't pushed, he'll spend his last hour in that same bed . . .*

• *Coyotes have found him and are pushing him all the way to Mexico . . .*

I didn't sleep more than two hours that night. And when morning came, I couldn't get dressed in my Mossy Oaks fast enough. Ranch owner B. J. Carothers and my friend Gene Braziel joined Don and I as we drove to the backside of the ranch to look for the big buck. Sure enough, we hadn't gone fifty yards into the thicket before we spotted a huge rack jutting up from the rocky ground.

The camera angle had fooled us. The arrow had actually pierced both lungs and exited in the perfect spot. The buck had been running dead and probably didn't last one minute after the arrow passed through. This thought comforted me, and I thanked the Good Lord for the biggest buck of my life during my first forty-three years of hunting.

I slept like a rock the following night.

ONE MORE DAY

You can relate to the "night before" syndrome. Whether you're a child trying to go to sleep on Christmas Eve, or a turkey hunter who's roosted a double-bearded gobbler in the old oak tree and you know the odds are finally in your favor the next morning, the night before is one filled with anticipation, excitement, and even a bit of anxiety that the alarm clock might malfunction.

But let's think about another "night before" experience—the night before your death. Yes, you read it correctly—your death.

You and I are going to die.

The Bible says it this way: "It is appointed for people to die once—and after this, judgment" (Hebrews 9:27).

Have you ever thought much about that? My good friend Marty Roe, lead singer for the country music group Diamond Rio, sings a popular song called "One More Day" that suggests a similar thought. People across the world have embraced this song, being moved to tears because of loved ones who have died, people they would love to spend just "one more day" with.

What if you knew you only had one more day to live? Would you do anything different? Would you make some specific phone calls? Would you write a letter? Would you say anything special to your children or your wife? Would you get your house in order? Would you forgive someone?

How would you react on the night before your death if you knew it was coming the next day?

ONE LAST NIGHT

Something that has really helped me deal with the reality of my own impending death is the fact that Jesus Himself experienced it. He knew better than anyone else the anxiety associated with the "night before" one's death.

Most of us will never know we're experiencing our last night on earth, so we'll probably be spared that particular anxiety. *Jesus wasn't.* He knew something most of us don't know. He knew exactly when and how he was going to die.

He knew that the very next day he would be whipped, beaten, spit upon, and mocked, a crown of thorns hammered into His skull. He was fully aware He would be nailed to a cross. That's why we find Him in the Garden of Gethsemane during the dark hours of the night, unable to sleep even though His friends couldn't stay awake to comfort him. He fell on his face, crying out, begging his Father God to let it be any other way than the cross.

Luke, a medical doctor, is the only one of the four biographers of Jesus to mention that Jesus sweated drops of blood (Luke 22:44). Dr. Luke may have been pointing to a rare but documented medical occurrence called *hematadrosis*, where there is so much anxiety that the brain swells and bursts the capillaries in the subject's forehead, causing blood to seep through the pores and mix with sweat, placing the subject in a mild state of shock.

Why did Jesus beg to get out of such suffering, yet then go on to say, "Not My will, but Yours be done"? (Luke 22:42). Why did He willingly subject Himself to such anxiety, humiliation, and torture? The answer is simple yet profound: He loves you so much, He wanted to save you from the fear of death!

Jesus knew that after the suffering, after being abandoned by His Father God because of the sins of the world He was bearing on the cross (including my sins and yours), peace and joy would reign. He could see beyond death to the Resurrection. He knew His Father would return to rescue Him and raise Him up. He was fully aware that Satan ultimately loses the war, even though in our lives Satan may have won a few battles *within* the war. Jesus lived with a vision beyond death.

You and I can do the same.

ONE BRIGHT HOPE

Death is not something to be dreaded by a Christian. It's actually more of a transition from one world to another, from the physical world we call earth to the spiritual world known as heaven.

Though our earth suit ceases to function in the event of our death, our spirit lives on for eternity, never growing old and weak. The essence of who we truly are is our spiritual being, for it is made in the image of the Creator. We don't have to fear death because Jesus has already conquered death for us. We can already know for a fact that we have eternal life (see 1 John 5:11–13).

JESUS LIVED WITH A VISION BEYOND DEATH. YOU AND I CAN DO THE SAME.

Just the opposite is true if we *aren't* God-followers. Death is the most dreaded nightmare a man could ever face if he's not a Christian, because although he, too, will have an eternal existence, the location and outcome will be hell itself, where he will spend all eternity knowing he had a chance and blew it, feeling the separation anxiety of being away from God, away from all he holds dear.

God knows the death date for every person on earth, both Christians and non-Christians alike. He knows *your* death date. He'll be thinking about it the night before it happens, your last night on earth. He'll know if you're walking in a relationship with Him or not, and He'll be aware that the next day holds something either incredible for you as you make the transition from earth to heaven, or that the day is literally going to be "hell" for you.

Sure, it's natural to cling to life on earth. You have people and things you love. You've grown attached to your body and the experiences you enjoy, including time in the outdoors. You want to see your kids or your grandkids grow up and do well. You want to spend more time with the people you love, see places you haven't seen, do things you haven't done.

But all of this is placed in proper perspective when you remember that the greatest adventure of all is yet to be lived, that the greatest relationship you can ever experience is yet to be fully developed—spending eternity with God in heaven.

REFLECT

Think about a "night before" experience in your own hunting or fishing career that caused you a restless night. Record your experience in the field journal below:

LOOK AT THE BOOK

The Old Testament book of Genesis records a story about a couple named Abraham and Sarah. God had promised that they would be the chosen lineage through which He would raise up a great nation called Israel.

God promised them a son, but they were well past the age of childbearing. Abraham was 99 and Sarah was 90. But God worked a miracle, and the next thing you know, Sarah was waddling along with a pickle in one hand and an ice cream cone in the other.

Soon Isaac was born to them as the firstborn heir. Abraham and Sarah were so proud of their new son. He was the seed line for the great nation of the prophecy.

Then something happened. The story is told in Genesis 22:1–3.

After these things God tested Abraham and said to him, "Abraham!"

"Here I am," he answered.

"Take your son," He said, "your only son Isaac, whom you love, go to the land of Moriah, and offer him there as a burnt offering on one of the mountains I will tell you about."

So early the next morning Abraham got up, saddled his donkey, and took with him two of his young men and his son Isaac. He split wood for a burnt offering and set out to go to the place God had told him about.

Did you notice the phrase "early the next morning"? Abraham had to experience the "night before" syndrome in a way you and I cannot relate to. I seriously doubt he went to bed. If he did, he probably didn't sleep at all. Only God Himself can truly understand Abraham's pain of heart—the deep, gut-wrenching agony that comes from knowing that the next day, your only son is going to be killed.

Do you think Isaac knew what was going on? What about Sarah? If so, what do you think was going through their minds?

DIG DEEPER

1. What are the similarities and differences between Isaac and Jesus in this story? (You'll need to read the remainder of Genesis 22 to get the whole picture.)

Similarities   *Differences*

2. Now do the same exercise between Abraham and God:

Similarities   *Differences*

FROM THE HEART

1. Death will come for every person, including you. Some day you will get up for the last time, eat one final meal, make one final phone call, and say goodbye to your family one last time. If you knew that you had only twenty-four hours left to live, what things would you do differently today? (List them in order of priority.)

2. The most important question of all: Would you do anything different spiritually? If so, what?

POSTSCRIPT

A relationship with God demands that we accept Jesus Christ as the only Lord and Savior and be obedient to His teachings. His will becomes our will. His ways become our ways. These are serious things we're talking about. Let's get serious about it together.

THE MOMENT OF TRUTH

Visualization.

It's kind of a new age word of sorts. You see the bumper stickers those bleeding hearts have crafted which say, "Visualize world peace." I suppose the postmodern thinking behind this stuff is that if you visualize it, you can achieve it.

Now, I don't believe you can visualize peace and then achieve it. Peace can only come through the Prince of Peace, Jesus Christ. But while I don't believe in *that* kind of visualization, I'm a firm believer that visualization can help tremendously when it comes to hunting. (So perhaps we're talking about two different types of visualization!)

The type of visualization I mean is athletically based, not spiritually based. Most all the athletes I know use some sort of visualization techniques when it comes to their performance.

The idea is simple: Practice like you play.

Practice being under pressure. Imagine yourself on the free-throw line with no time left on the clock. When you're practicing your putting stroke in the living room late one weeknight, imagine you're standing over a four-footer for the city championship title.

Hunting is no different. You must add some fantasy into the practice time if you want to prepare yourself for the moment of truth.

PREPARED FOR SUCCESS

A few years ago I got in the habit of practicing from a tree stand when shooting my bow. My friend Max and I had hung a stand in his back yard, which was wooded and had the ultimate set up for practicing like you play. We would set up about four to five 3D targets and take turns retrieving for one another. We created all kinds of scenarios and opportunities to provide the greatest amount of realism possible.

We did quartering-toward-you shots. Shooting straight down at a deer's spine. Deer tucked behind trees. Even thirty-five yard shots through the woods (which is a whopping lot different than thirty-five yards in an open field). We practiced holding for long periods of time before releasing. We did it all—even going so far as to snorting at the shooter without warning him!

And man, am I glad we went through all of that, because it paid off tremendously for me just a few weeks later during archery hunting season.

It was mid-October, and the deer were still somewhat predictable. I was hunting one of my favorite bow hunting spots—a little, hidden location on a small farm that has one of the biggest persimmon trees I've ever known to exist.

(Actually, it was two persimmon trees which split at the base. They went up about sixty feet like two tall towers full of fruit.) Every persimmon tree I've ever seen or heard of was shorter and bent over from the weight of the persimmons. Not this beauty. And man, did it ever bring in the deer!

READY FOR ACTION

One frosty morning around 8:00, I caught movement in my right eye. Two bucks were walking right to me on a worn-out trail, and I was perched only ten yards from that persimmon. To be honest, I really should have been a little farther off the red zone than I was, but the trees in that vicinity would have put me either too far away or would've offered no shot. I had to be this close, and I could get away with it because I was hunting from about twenty-five feet.

Having suffered from last season's withdrawals of going deerless with my bow, this buck offered me some redemption. Though he was no Pope & Young stalwart, I was not going to let him pass.

He came in directly under my stand, stopping ever so slightly, quartering toward me at only six yards. I had an awesome look at his vitals from that high up, but the angle was steep. "That's good enough," I thought to myself—because I'd seen this same scenario before . . . in practice sessions with Max.

MY CONFIDENCE IN THAT SHOT CAME FROM THE REALISM OF BEING PREPARED FOR IT BOTH MENTALLY AND PHYSICALLY.

I drew my bow, and the buck looked straight up at me. The arrow flew. From that distance he took the full and complete brunt of my arrow flying at maximum speed. He ran about fifteen yards and flipped heels over head. Never flinched. I think he was dead before he hit the ground.

My confidence in that shot came from the realism of being prepared for it both mentally and physically. Perhaps I run the risk of stating the obvious by admitting that I now practice this way every season!

Hunters should practice the way they play.

REFLECT

We all know the "perfect shot" for any archer—broadside slightly quartering away. Whether you're a bow hunter or gun hunter, what is the one shot you will not take even if it's open and why?

_____

_____

_____

_____

_____

_____

_____

LOOK AT THE BOOK

Everyone who competes in the games goes into strict training.—1 Corinthians 9:25 (NIV)

We live in a modern age were people everywhere are concerned about physical fitness. But what about *spiritual* fitness? Paul tells us that he disciplined himself . . . spiritually.

If there's one truth I've learned about sin, it's this: you don't win the battle with temptation if you're not prepared. The secret to winning the war with temptation is *predetermining the outcome of the battle!*

Let's say you're just surfing the Internet and you misspell the name of a Web site for power tools. And what appears before your eyes next is not a nail gun but a naked woman.

Now, you never meant to go there. All you did was type what you thought were the right letters and hit the enter key. See, porn sites do that to you. They're set up with fake domain names so that kids (or men) can accidentally wind up there and get drawn in.

Okay. Here you are, faced with a situation. How are you going to respond?

The key to success here is being prepared. And the time to prepare is NOT when you're in the moment of battle but before the battle ever begins! You tune the instrument before the concert, not when the concert gets underway!

The time to prepare for the battle is when you're levelheaded and unemotional, not when your heart is beating fast with temptation. It's in that time that you make a covenant with yourself that if you get on that computer today, and by chance you should encounter a porn site, you will immediately back out.

No hesitation. No long looks. Immediately!

Let me tell you—it works. And it works for more than just porn. It works over the business lunch when you're asked to fudge on your prices just to win a contract. If you've predetermined that you will not lie in the moment of truth, you'll win the battle. But if you're not prepared, you may give in, because you waited until the moment of truth to try and make a rational decision.

You cannot be rational if your mind and heart are being bombarded with all of Satan's arsenal. You must be instinctive.

DIG DEEPER

When a big buck hears a noise he's not familiar with, he doesn't wait to check it out. He bolts. Automatically. It doesn't matter if he understands it or knows what it is. He doesn't *need* to understand it. He immediately associates it with danger and he's outta there. Fast!

Get the idea? Where have you been guilty of hanging around too long? What has it cost you to be caught lingering, checking out temptation?

FROM THE HEART

1. Especially if you're working through this chapter in a small group study, discuss the differences between these preferences:

- helical or straight fletchings?
- feathers or plastic?
- fixed broadheads or mechanical?
- carbon, aluminum, or wood?
- rope release, fingers, or mechanical release?
- kisser or peep?
- long bow, recurve, or compound?
- Ford or Chevy?

2. What do you think Dallas Willard is getting at when he says: "A baseball player who expects to excel in the game without adequate exercise of his body is no more ridiculous than the Christian who hopes to be able to act in the manner of Christ when put to the test without the appropriate exercise in godly living."

POSTSCRIPT

Life is not a dry run, and good things don't just happen . . . in hunting or in anything else. Wonder what you could set in motion today if you gave it everything you had?

MID-SEASON

The grass withers, the flowers fade,
but the word of our God remains forever.

Isaiah 40:8

The mark of a great hunter is the ability to adapt and
explore new possibilities. There's also that constant
struggle of being born to hunt and forced to work!
While you're on the job, you find your mind often
drifting to varying scenarios of where he might be.
Has he shifted his morning route to another canyon
to stay closer to his cows? Has he changed bedding
areas because he's a whitetail and he's not going
to put up with too much pressure? Questions rarely
lead to answers, just to more questions.
That's why they call it hunting.

HUNTIN' BUDDIES

The old longbeard was as smart as a calculator. He knew just where to draw the line, staying beyond the edge of shotgun range by a beard's length. He strutted back and forth, just over the rise of the oak forest in the north Arkansas Ozarks.

My huntin' buddy Ted Jones and I had begun working the ancient gobbler at 12:15 p.m. As I glanced at my watch, I saw that fifty-five minutes had passed. After throwing out every hen call known to man and bird, and receiving a hundred gobbles in response, I knew this old bird was not coming any closer. Twice he had sent a hen in to check us out. She had returned on both occasions to report that there was nothing to be seen.

This old gobbler was the ultimate example of "hung up."

Have you ever been in a situation like this? If you're hunting alone, you really only have three options at this point: (1) try to move closer and probably spook the bird, (2) back out quietly and relocate for the next series of calls, or (3) sneak away and try him again on another occasion. Staying put just isn't going to get it done.

When you're *tag-teaming* a gobbler, however, a situation like the one described above can sometimes turn out in your favor.

Consider what Ted and I did.

BAIT AND SWITCH

I motioned to Ted that he should stay put and have his gun up and ready. I began to belly-crawl away from the gobbler, offering soft clucks and yelps with my mouth call as I went. The leaves were making plenty of noise under my weight, sounding like a turkey feeding along through the woods. I gave some soft contented feeding purrs. Old gobble-head rattled again and again, as I anticipated. I just kept crawling away.

Finally, after going about seventy yards behind Ted, I leaned against a tree and got ready for my next move. I took out two Knight and Hale fighting purr boxes, a Woods Wise Viper mouth call, and a gobble tube. I also retrieved the two turkey wings that I keep in my vest. Then I commenced to creating the biggest turkey fight between three jakes that has ever echoed through the Ozark Mountains.

I kicked leaves, beat wings against each other, and fought with the hand and mouth calls for one full minute. When I finally stopped, I grabbed the gobble tube and gave it a shake. Then I sat perfectly still, listening to the old gobbler triple-gobbling. I imagined in my mind what might be happening just out of my view as Ted sat ready with his shotgun shouldered.

It wasn't long until I heard the shot and the shout. The old gobbler had fallen to one of the most deadly tricks in a turkey hunter's book. He had sent his hen to check out the fight. She walked right past Ted and was continuing to my new location. The longbeard had followed, topping the ridge that had been hiding him, yet still careful to stay quite a ways back from the hen. He would let *her* find out if there were any dangers lurking further in the woods.

Little did he know that Ted was silently waiting, now inside the old bird's safety zone.

TWO ARE BETTER THAN ONE

I'll be the first to admit that I love to spend time alone in the outdoors. I like my private time. Part of me can connect with the old Robert Redford movie character, Jeremiah Johnson.

Yet at the same time, I love companionship as well. There's nothing like having a good buddy with me—or for that matter, having several buddies with me—to share in the experience. Maybe this is because I was created as a tribal creature.

The same is true for you. God intended from the very beginning for humans to live in community. If this weren't the case, He never would

GOD INTENDED FROM THE VERY BEGINNING FOR HUMANS TO LIVE IN COMMUNITY.

have created Eve for Adam. God made mankind with an innate desire for companionship.

If you don't believe that, just take a look at society. How many clubs or social groups can you find in your own hometown? I compiled a list from one small town where I used to live, and was quite surprised at the number of groups that had been formed:

- Quilting club. Kiwanis club. Rotary club.
- Boy Scouts. Girl Scouts. Cub Scouts.
- Bowling league. Baseball league. Soccer league.
- Bass fishing club. Archery club. National Wild Turkey Federation chapter.
- Parents of Disabled Children. Disabled Veterans of America. Daughters of the American Revolution.
- Alcoholics Anonymous. Tough Love parenting group. Knights of Columbus. Elks club.
- Toastmasters club. Sierra club. Remote Control Airplane club. And on and on.

God created humans to live within community with one another, sharing in one another's lives on a daily basis. That's why He established the church.

OUT ON YOUR OWN

Occasionally I run across someone who claims he's a Christian but isn't part of any fellowship or church. This is what I call Crocodile Dundee religion. In the movie bearing the same name,

Paul Hogan's character says, "Me and God are mates"—("mytes," to hear it in his accent)—insinuating that his church was nothing more than the outback of Australia. People would just mess it up, I guess. He didn't need people.

Maybe you can relate. Maybe you think you and God are enough. You don't need people, especially hypocrites to mess it all up. You can go it alone spiritually—Jeremiah Johnson style.

If this is what you believe, try an experiment. Make a fire and let it burn for a while. Once you get some hot coals glowing in the fire, reach in with a stick and pull one of the coals out a few feet away from the fire, then just sit back and watch what happens to the coal. It'll begin to lose its glow, putting out less and less heat until it eventually burns out.

And that's exactly what happens to a person who removes himself from the fellowship of the church.

If this has happened to you, take a lesson from the coal. The only way to get it glowing again is to put it back with the other coals that are hot.

That's the way it is with the church. You and I need the church, hypocrites and all.

LIFE IN COMMUNITY

God created us to live in community—to walk the trail of life together, to draw strength from one another, to share with one another, to hold one another accountable, to encourage one another, to laugh and cry together. Trust me, it's much easier to climb a mountain tethered to other skilled climbers than to try climbing it alone. When you fall, someone's there to catch you. When someone else falls, you're there to help him. That's the way life is supposed to work.

Hunters, of all people, should know this.

Whether it's tag-teaming on a gobbler, doing a deer drive, flushing pheasants for the shooters at the end of the row, teasing in a cobia with a jig so the fly fisherman can have a chance with the fly, or simply working in tandem to follow a blood trail, there's just something special about having a huntin' buddy along for the trip.

IT'S THE WAY OF COLLECTIVE WISDOM—A WISDOM OF THE GROUP THAT'S GREATER THAN THE WISDOM OF ONE.

The same is true for the spiritual life.

Every man needs a group of men with whom he can walk through the adventure of life. You and I need an accountability group—a group of men that will ask us the hard questions like:

- "Are you staying faithful to your wife?"
- "How are you doing with that addiction you're trying to kick?"
- "Are you spending both quality and quantity time with your kids?"
- "Have you looked at any form of Internet porn this week?"
- "How's your walk with God going lately?"

Having a few good men in our lives to walk with us through this earthly journey is the safest way to live. It's the way of collective wisdom—a wisdom of the group that's greater than the wisdom of the individual. It's the way of warriors who battle back to back in the heat of the moment. It's the way of huntin' buddies who know one another so well they're already anticipating the next move.

ALL TOGETHER NOW

I am so thankful for the three men with whom I serve on the pastoral team of New River Fellowship in Franklin, Tennessee.

Raphael Giglio is an Italian Messianic Jew who has never hunted in his life. He looks like he could have just stepped off the set of *Miami Vice.*

Colin Campbell is a New Zealander transplanted in America. He speaks with an Aussie accent and drives his old tractor with his tie on.

Michael W. Smith is a Grammy Award-winning singer/songwriter and an artist in every sense of the word. Most of the time he leads worship while wearing sandals.

I'm the guy with the beard, boots, and the branded Bible.

Individually each one of us is very different. Yet when we come together on a weekly basis, there's a bond between us. Our differences of personality, perspective, and experience

THE LIFE BEST LIVED IS THE LIFE LIVED IN COMMUNITY WITH OTHERS.

serve as strengths that combine for a collective wisdom far greater than any of us could muster alone. Our collective experience in walking God's trail combines to 180 years, far beyond the years that any of us will live individually.

We pray together, cry together, laugh together, work together, play together, plan together, go on dates together with our wives, celebrate one another's birthdays, and hold each other accountable. Such is the nature of walking God's trail with a group of men who love you unconditionally and who would most likely take a bullet for you.

You need such men in your life.

WIDEN YOUR CIRCLE

It's also important, however, to move out beyond your closed group of warriors and invite others into your life adventure.

When I think back to some of my favorite memories from the woods, I think of my friend, Coach Jeff Fisher, harvesting his first turkey. (He actually killed two longbeards with one shot by accident!) He was more excited on that spring morning, I believe, than when his Tennessee Titans pulled off the "Music City Miracle" in the NFL playoffs!

I think of Gary LeVox, lead singer for Rascal Flatts, as we walked down a woods road and talked about what God means to us, while Gary's nine-point bruiser buck hung back at the shed.

I remember eating sandwiches with Harold Knight in his turkey blind and shooting a longbeard he called in an hour later.

And then there were the two days with Phil Robertson—the "Duck Commander"—as we "cut 'em all, Jack" and did lots of "God talk."

Add to these experiences the time I saw Steve Chapman, author of *A Look at Life from a Deer Stand*, take his biggest buck with a bow.

I'll never forget coaching my son Jonathan as he got his first bow kill, and being present when my wife, Amanda, took her first racked buck. I will always cherish sitting side-by-side with my dad when he shot a Saskatchewan trophy whitetail of a lifetime, and being in camp when my daughter Christin snapped a 35 mm photo of two bucks fighting. Her grin was a mile wide. Mine was wider when she showed me the picture.

Imagine if I had not shared my time in God's great outdoors with these huntin' buddies, including my own family members? I would've missed out on so much. On some of these occasions, we weren't even successful at harvesting any animals, yet the hunt was a great success because of the relationships that were strengthened.

Once again, the same is true spiritually.

Are you sharing your life adventure with others who are making you a better person? Do you have any huntin' buddies, or are you living your life out of rhythm because you're trying to go it alone?

Remember, the life best lived is the life lived in community with others.

REFLECT

1. Think back to the wise old gobbler Jimmy and Ted tag-teamed. Have you ever experienced success in the woods because of the buddy system? Record your experience in the field journal below.

_____

_____

_____

_____

_____

_____

_____

2. Jimmy mentioned an experiment of taking a red-hot coal from a fire and watching it. What's the main point he's trying to make with this analogy?

_____

_____

_____

_____

_____

_____

_____

_____

LOOK AT THE BOOK

Fifty days after the death and resurrection of Jesus in the first century AD, a special Jewish feast took place in Jerusalem. People from long distances traveled there each year to participate in this feast called Pentecost (meaning "Fifty days after Passover").

God chose this day to establish His church, a church that would eventually include not only Jews but also Gentiles. He used some men who were Jesus' closest followers (some diehard fishermen) to speak a message in every language represented in the audience. And the response was incredible! Three thousand people yielded themselves to Jesus, claimed Him as the only Lord of their lives, and were baptized that same day, being "added" to the church (Acts 2:47).

A doctor named Luke wrote about these events in a letter now known as "Acts of the Apostles." Within this letter Luke described the new members of God's church:

They devoted themselves to the apostles' teaching, to fellowship, to the breaking of bread, and to prayers.... All the believers were together and had everything in common. So they sold their possessions and property and distributed the proceeds to all, as anyone had a need. And every day they devoted themselves to meeting together in the temple complex, and broke bread from house to house. They ate their food with gladness and simplicity of heart, praising God and having favor with all the people" (Acts 2:42, 44–47)

DIG DEEPER

In the Bible text that you just read, some key themes and phrases emerge describing the early Christians. They were:

- devoted to one another
- filled with love for one another
- together daily
- bonded with one another
- sold personal possessions to help one another
- shared meals in one another's homes
- prayed together
- praised God together

Clearly the early Christians did more than just go to church on Sunday morning or Wednesday night. It appears that religion was a 24/7 commitment not only to God but also to one another.

Do you have a "community" of people you're this committed to? If so, describe what it's like. If not, try to think through why you don't.

FROM THE HEART

On a scale of 1 to 10, rate how well the community to which you are committed helps you draw closer to God on a daily basis. (Circle your answer.)

1 . . . 2 . . . 3 . . . 4 . . . 5 . . . 6 . . . 7 . . . 8 . . . 9 . . . 10

Are you interested in becoming part of a community of believers—Christians who share a commitment to Jesus Christ as Lord? If so, you might start by reading Luke's letter recorded in the New Testament—Acts of the Apostles. There you will find many stories about men and women who made the same decision. This may help you know what kind of community to look for in your own geographical area.

If you are already a member of a church but would like to grow a close-knit community of outdoorsmen with whom you can walk together in the adventure of life, you might try starting an outdoors-related Bible class. You can have activities such as wild game suppers, archery tournaments, family fishing days, and so forth, during which you can add a spiritual element. If you need some ideas, feel free to contact us through our Web site at *www.SpiritualOutdoorAdventures.org*. We would also be happy to supply you with over a year's worth of curriculum for your classes.

Remember, becoming a Christian doesn't just bring you into a relationship with God. It also brings you into a relationship with many other people who become your brothers and sisters in Christ.

POSTSCRIPT

Ironically, you can never truly go hunting alone. God, the greatest Hunter of all, is with you always, wherever you go.

WOUNDED

I don't think I will ever be able to erase this memory.

It was late December and I guess I was feeling cocky. I wanted to put a stalk on a whitetail with my bow. (I live in Tennessee, and in our state you can basically bow hunt from late September to early January with virtually no break in the action.) The chance of this thing coming together, though, was slim and none . . . and slim was on his way out of town! Even still, *What if?* That's what pulled me into the woods that day.

I have access to a farm that reminds me of the terrain out west. The lush acreage has it all when it comes to favorable spot and stalk conditions. High grassy ridges with fence rows. Tree lines that crisscross the property. Hollows with big timber. Fields with sage grass to hide in.

So there I was in December, bow in hand. Camera and tripod, too, were bound tightly to my pack. The sun was fighting for its share of space between the fast moving clouds. A front was coming in later that night, the barometer was dropping, and it was just now starting to snow. The wind was howling a cold bite that could chew through bone.

Certifiably crazy, I was. Should have been home watching football. I'd already taken a really nice buck that season, but one thing loomed in my mind: you cannot create a memory from the couch! (Yeah, but you can dang sure dream about one without the agony and risk of frostbite!)

Even still, *What if?*

IS HE OR ISN'T HE?

Not fifteen minutes from the truck, wind slapping me straight in the face like a bullwhip on steroids, I stood high atop a canyon ridge glassing my favorite tree line.

My optics magnetically tilted toward a cinnamon spot just along the edge where the oaks met the sloping field edge. A deer raised its head. *Wow! Right out of the gate and into the action!*

It was a doe (I thought), which was good enough for me on this hunt. The stalk was what I had come for. On second look, though, I realized I was wrong. It was a buck—and from what I could tell, a really tall six-pointer.

Something didn't seem quite right about him to me, however. For one thing, his coat stood out tremendously. Usually deer get really washed out in gray this time of year, but he was a bright cinnamon color. Odd.

Also, for some reason he stood totally motionless for about three minutes, which gave me time to take in the elements, engineer potential sneak routes, factor the wind, and craft all the other necessary thoughts that would go into this hunt. But having no desire to shoot a smaller buck, I was quickly coming to the conclusion that I'd just keep looking for a doe.

Then everything changed.

He tried to take a step, and I saw at an instant that he had no use of his back left leg. None at all. He'd been shot in probably the worst of all non-lethal regions on his body. That was why he had stayed motionless for so long. He was just storing up energy to move the next five feet.

My heart literally sank. Honest it did. Right into my gut. I felt real pain in my soul for this fella. *Of all the days to leave my rifle at home,* I thought. *I could end this right now!* Instantly I decided—for his sake alone—to attempt to get close enough for a shot, to end his misery. I'd never seen a deer hurt this badly.

It bothers me, you see. And it bothers me on many levels.

COME OUT FIRING

For starters, I cannot for the life of me under-stand why veteran hunters insist on continually shooting small bucks. Perhaps I should retract my words and say that I *do* understand it, but I just can't agree with it. I believe it's a pride thing—a super hostile takeover where the ego attacks the brain and destroys every ounce of common sense left in the hunter's mind.

Guys love horns. (Hey, so do I, but not *little* horns!) Any hunter worth his salt would admit that there's more challenge in trying to get close to an old doe than a young, ignorant buck. Yet hunters in basically every state consistently shoot small bucks and then complain that their hunting areas don't produce big deer.

So a hunter sees horns, gets excited, and starts slingin' lead. Sometimes he connects, sometimes he doesn't. And sometimes he connects without killing the buck, only to ruin that deer's chance of ever reaching maturity, dooming him to a short life when he could've been a majestic trophy in only two more years. That's why it bothers me so much.

HE COULD HAVE BEEN A MAJESTIC TROPHY IN ONLY TWO MORE YEARS.

Where's the glory in shooting your 37th five-pointer? In fact, I can't tell you how many times I've talked with hunters who have told me how excited they were to be traveling to south Texas this year, or that they hoped they were drawn on the lottery for their Kansas tag because, "That's where you've got to go if you want to shoot a big one!"

In many ways these guys are right. Kansas, Iowa, Illinois, Nebraska, and south Texas do hold huge whitetails on a larger ratio than the Southeastern states, but mainly because hunters keep poppin' the little fellas! If hunters in the

Southeast would take more does and let some small bucks grow, you'd never hear of a hunter leaving his state to hunt elsewhere for any reason other than simply wanting a change in scenery!

GROW UP!

For all you hunters who do let small bucks walk, I thank you. (And I thank you a second time for putting up with my last few moments of preaching.)

Of course, I've got nothing at all against someone taking a smaller buck when it's his first deer. That's a great moment. My first deer was a half-rack three-pointer that may as well have been a 150-class wall-hanger! When my son, Cole, grows into hunting age, I'll be as happy as can be with his first deer, whether buck or doe.

But the other reason harvesting small bucks bothers me so much is because it's just plain bad management.

In my early years of whitetail hunting, you never dreamed of taking a doe. It just wasn't the thing to do. Then again, we didn't have anywhere near the knowledge of game management we do now. The secret isn't a secret anymore: keeping the doe population down means that only your bigger bucks are breeding the available does, which passes on better genetics. I know of some intensely managed ranches where the owners force the guides to harvest several does per man before they can start guiding for the season!

But I have a confession to make: I've struggled with being willing to harvest does myself. It's just so different from the way I started hunting. Yet the truth remains that many states are suffering from overcrowded populations, and doe harvests are the answer. That's why I accept the call and harvest does, because it's every hunter's responsibility.

ONE FINAL STALK

Here I was, staring down this nice six-pointer who probably wasn't going to make it through the winter, and I was angry. *Why couldn't the guy just let him walk?* Perhaps it was a young boy shooting at his first whitetail. *That's what I'd like to think!*

Keeping the wind in my face, I banked hard left to get into the tree line. I had to walk 200 yards down a steep wooded hollow, up the other side, and then cross a small meadow just to get on his level. I estimated it would take me an hour just to get within fifty yards of him. Sunset would be in an hour and a half.

I had no time to lose.

I successfully made it down the hollow and up the other side without having my cover blown. The wind that was howling so loudly was my friend on this day. I was about seventy-five yards away with a meadow separating me from my wounded challenge, and I could no longer get a visual on him. *Had he moved?* Surely not. He was so hurt, there's no way he could be far.

Just then I saw his head close to the ground. He had only moved about thirty yards in that last forty-five minutes! Oh, how I wanted this to come together—for his sake, sure, but also because it would still be a super hunt with a bow. I crawled on my hands and knees through the sage grass, putting some brush between us, giving him no way of seeing me. The last fifty yards would be critical, though. There was a knoll separating us, so I couldn't see him *either*. But I knew he was on the other side.

As I inched along in the sage grass, my mind raced trying to figure out how I would ever get the camera set up on him. My only hope was that he was bedded down so I'd have time to go slow.

As I hit what I estimated to be the forty-yard barrier, I realized that I could no longer crawl. I was approaching the tree line, and the frozen leaves were going to make too much noise. I knew what had to be done. I was going to have to take off my boots and do a Geronimo stalk!

Adrenaline is a funny thing. I never even noticed my freezing toes! Taking a step every thirty seconds, I finally made my way to where I could barely see over the wooded rise.

He wasn't there.

What? He couldn't be far! I'd marked a big oak tree from where I'd last seen him, and I was now standing right beside it.

But six steps and sixty seconds later, I saw him. And he saw me. He hobbled away at an incredibly slow pace, and I knew it was over. I wasn't going to push him. If I'd had my rifle, I could've taken him in a second, but I couldn't dare force him to expend whatever bit of energy he had left just because I was taking a risky shot with a bow.

I've never been flooded with that many conflicting emotions. My heart sank, because I wanted to offer him mercy from a slow death. Yet every hunter would understand when I say that my face bore a smile fresh from an extraordinary memory of a hunt on a snowy December day.

HEART WOUNDS

I think you and I have a common connection with that wounded buck. We've all wounded our share of animals. I've done it. It's a sickening feeling that only hunters know.

Yet if you live more than a minute on earth, you'll receive your wounds. Many wounds. Sin has done that to all of us. Adam faced it. Eve experienced it. We are well aware of our transgressions, and we wear the scars to prove it.

Paul, that great apostle, had a history of violence and hatred. Samson let a woman get the best of him. In a fit of volcanic anger, Moses lost his livelihood as he once knew it. Noah, a guy who had more faith in God than any man of his day, got so drunk that he passed out naked, shaming his entire family. David, after breaking covenant with his wife and chasing another woman into bed, finally dealt with his horror. "I know my transgressions," he said (Ps. 51:3, NIV).

Can't you hear the familiarity in his voice? He was well aware of the ways he'd brought shame into his life. He was intimately connected with the skeletal makeup of the bones in his closet.

Sometimes our sins bring great shame. Sometimes they just bring embarrassment. But either way, the wounds are there, and we know them. Like memories branded into the hide of our minds, we have a hard time finding a new identity with any other owner.

Yet you and I have a different option than that of a wounded animal. We have a way out. A wounded animal must accept his fate. Fate, however, doesn't apply to the believer, for we live in Christ.

We can look to Him and be healed.

REFLECT

How big of an issue to you are some of the hunting dilemmas Jason talked about in this chapter?

LOOK AT THE BOOK

When you were dead in trespasses . . . He made you alive with Him and forgave us all our transgressions. He erased the certificate of debt, with its obligations, that was against us and opposed to us, and has taken it out of the way by nailing it to the cross.
—Colossians 2:13–14

Playing alongside Tom Hanks in *The Green Mile*, the mystical character John Coffey could heal people. Cancer, death, pain—it made no difference. No matter what their horrible situation, he could heal it. Referring to their pain and his willingness to deal with it, he would offer them healing, often saying, "I took it back."

Jesus Christ holds no active profile with the Screen Actors Guild. He is not a mythical figure made up by a Hollywood screen writer. He lived in an historical moment in time, and He still lives today.

And He alone really can take it back!

He knows your failures and trangressions, and he can take them away. You don't have to live out your days in pain. You don't have to make the best of a bad situation. By God's own words, if you are in Christ, you are a "new creation" (2 Cor. 5:17). New. Not repaired, not mended—new!

For just a minute, contrast Peter and Judas. (Read about them in Matthew 26:69–27:10). Both of these men let God down in a major way. In fact, their sins were of the worst kind—public!

Yet the difference between Peter and Judas was simple: Peter repented and dealt with his sins, and Judas did not. Peter moved on with his life, but Judas took his. Peter moved out in the open and kept going ahead in God's forgiveness. Judas hid himself, but he couldn't hide from his heart, so he killed himself.

The lesson is clear: deal with your sins, or they will deal with you.

DIG DEEPER

What is it about your deepest wounds, your deepest sins, that makes you so mad at yourself?

_____

_____

_____

Why do you think you've held on to them this long without recovering from them?

_____

_____

_____

You know you've wounded others, too. Have you left those wounds open? How?

_____

_____

_____

FROM THE HEART

You know your transgressions well. But are you willing to deal with them? Healing is most certainly a process, but it can be complete. The question is, are you willing to start?

What is one action step you can take this week to move on as a new creature in Christ?

_____

_____

_____

I AM YOUR HORSE

Have you ever noticed how camouflage tends to fade over time, especially when it's put through the washer/dryer cycle? A wooden deer stand will do the same thing. No matter how big or how fresh the wood is when you build it, at some point in the future, that old stand is going to be rotten to the point you can no longer climb on it to hunt.

Such is the nature of living in an earth suit. Even the Bible acknowledges this, that "outwardly we are wasting away" (2 Cor. 4:16, NIV). This is a natural part of life. Bodies age. Stamina decreases. Eyes fade. Hearing goes away like the echo of a rifle shot. Eventually we die.

But if we're not careful, the same thing can happen to our hearts.

In outdoorsman John Eldredge's book *Waking the Dead*, the author makes the following point: "The single most unifying quality shared by all humans on planet earth today—we are all losing heart or we have already lost heart! That glorious image of God in us is fading like dye in a cotton shirt that is washed multiple times."

This statement reminds me of a four-year-old girl who was overhead whispering to her new baby brother while he lay in his crib the first night home from the hospital: "Baby brother, tell me what God is like. I'm starting to forget."

HEARTBREAK

We are born full of life. Full of heart. Ready to explore new things and conquer the world. Then as we age and go through the up and down experiences of life, we get tired, skeptical, cynical, lazy. The heart grows dull. We struggle to see clearly, like trying to look through thick fog along the river in early morning.

To some degree, you and I have all experienced the pain of a broken heart:

- The grief that comes from the death of someone close to you.
- The pain of divorce.
- The separation anxiety when your children leave home.
- The hurt when you get a pink slip or hear the words "You're fired."
- The anger you feel when you realize that someone you once respected has used you.
- The loneliness of being forgotten or overlooked.
- The letdown of promises unkept—maybe something as simple as "I'll call you," but they never do.
- The heart shattered by rejection.

- The bitterness you feel when your Christian brother or sister or pastor lets you down.
- The haunting memory of abuse from a parent when you were a child.
- The devastation you felt when your first girl-friend broke up with you.
- The hurtful memory of the time you were cut from the team and your best friend made it.
- The time your brother or sister made fun of one of your physical characteristics.
- The realization that you are not living your dream.

The list goes on and on. And sadly, the worst blows tend to come from those who know us well and should have loved us more.

These things tend to break off pieces of our heart, leaving it void of anything good, making room for bitterness, resentment, anger, revenge, unworthiness, and lack of trust to seep in, hardening us for the long haul, allowing nothing else in. As a result, we allow much of our heart to be stolen from us, and we end up living in resentment for the rest of our lives.

If this is you, I want you to take heart. I've been there. And I want to share with you a recent outdoor adventure that gave me some answers to the dilemma of my own broken heart.

THE IDAHO ADVENTURE

It happened in the high country of Idaho, where for ten days I lived in the Bitterroot Wilderness and followed the trail of the historic

Lewis and Clark expedition. Traveling along the Locksaw River, where salmon migrate several hundred miles from the Pacific Ocean, I joined a group of adventurers at base camp. We saddled up the horses (plus one very funny mule) and packed gear for a journey that would take us even deeper into the wilderness.

We began the two-hour ride to high camp, once again following the trail of the river and then winding our way upward on a switchback trail. We had twenty-two horses and mules in the pack train, and we eventually arrived at the high camp, which consisted of two tents and a make-shift corral.

Two outdoor legends were in camp with us. One was Paul Meaks, founder of API Industries as well as Great Day Incorporated. Paul can be seen on television's outdoor channels just about daily. The other was Jerry Peterson, creator of **WE BEGAN THE TWO-HOUR RIDE TO HIGH CAMP, WINDING OUR WAY UPWARD ON A SWITCH-BACK TRAIL.** the first marketed deer call. Jerry owns Woods Wise Callmasters Game Calls and has produced numerous outdoor videos.

With these two guys in camp and three cameras to capture the action, I knew we were in for an incredible taping of a *Spiritual Outdoor Adventures* episode. Bears and other game were plentiful in these mountains, and Lost Lakes Outfitters (owned by Philip Barrett) has a great reputation for putting hunters in the action.

We were bow hunting, and our main objective was to call in and harvest three bull elk. The budget for this episode was higher than usual, but we knew it would be worth it when the final edit was completed. You've heard the old saying, though: "The best laid plans of mice and men." That statement certainly applied to this trip.

For example, due to the re-introduction of wolves into the area we were hunting, the elk wouldn't bugle. As a result we couldn't find them. We heard one bull in eight days.

On top of that, the terrain was steep and thick as a rain forest, making walking extremely difficult. I fell numerous times, feeling as if I was in Special Forces boot camp. Paul's knees swelled up on him, confining him to hunting only from horseback. Even the bears were unusually skittish, staying back in the brush, picking us out on the stands we were hunting from.

So you can imagine what camp was like on the eve of the final day. Everyone was worn out and spirits were low. I crawled into my sleeping bag praying that God would come through for us. Tomorrow was all we had left.

LIFE ON THE TRAIL

The next morning our guide, Adam Reed, led my cameraman Don Belles and me on a long horseback ride to the highest mountain in the area. It was a two-hour ride from high camp.

When we arrived there, we tied off the horses and began a day's hike through the dense, rugged Idaho terrain. It was the toughest day of walking I've ever experienced.

At noon we stopped for sandwiches and ended up snoozing in a pocket of sunlight on the earth floor for a couple of hours. I couldn't sleep very well, so I took out my journal and began to write. Rather than focusing on our lack of success and the evident lack of a TV episode, I did some reflecting on things I had experienced during the week:

• I remembered the springs of cold, clear water gushing from the mountainside where I'd filled up my water bottle. These springs reminded me of Jesus' statement that He not only is the bread of life, but that He also has living water (see John 4:10–14).

• I remembered the majestic conifer trees that had lived a full life and had died, falling to the earth floor where they began to decompose. I witnessed this decomposition in its various stages, and even came upon new trees that were sprouting from the decaying remains. I was reminded that my body will go through the same process, that life is short, that there is an end to my physical existence. Yet I also realized that because of Christ's grace and salvation, I won't suffer the same fate as a downed tree. I will be resurrected from the grave! Life will come from my death! (see 1 Cor. 15:35–58).

• I remembered how tough it was to walk through the thick parts of the forest. Each step led to a potential fall. I ended up praying, "Lord, guide every step of my life. Make my path clear." That's a prayer I need to pray even when I'm back in the concrete jungle (see Ps. 18:32–36).

• I witnessed the beauty of God's mountains and remembered those incredible verses in the Bible that talk about them crying out to God, the trees singing to Him, how all of nature is a chorus to God and His majesty (see Ps. 98:7–9; 19:1–2).

• I walked through a burned-out forest where everything had been severely stripped by a blazing forest fire. Yet I noticed that green patches of grass were sprouting from the charred rubble. The heat from the fire had caused cones to open and release their seeds, thus giving birth to new trees. The fire had actually provided nutrients that were previously missing. Great growth was pending because of the fire. I remembered the concept of the refiner's fire in the Bible. Sometimes we have to go through fire in order to achieve growth (see Ps. 66:10–12).

SURPRISE, SURPRISE

I walked the rest of the day without hearing an elk bugle, forced to resign myself to the fact that in spite of the huge investment, I was going home without a show. That's what made the words of my guide, Adam, even harder to register in my brain when we finally arrived at night-fall—soaked with sweat and

THEY HAD SLIPPED THEIR BRIDLES AND HEADED BACK TO CAMP.

worn to a frazzle—at the place where we had tied the horses.

The two horses were gone. They had slipped their bridles and probably headed back to camp several miles away.

But to make things even worse, my new headlight had burned out. What an awful way to end a week—no elk, no show, no light. And now I was drenched in sweat and exhausted, with the temperatures falling fast, many miles away from camp down a treacherous slope, about to spend most of the night in the remote wilderness among wolves, cougars, and bears. *Great!*

Adam took off on his mule to ride back to camp and get some horses. But I knew it would be four hours before he could get back to us—not until 2 a.m. By the time we could start our long ride back to camp, we'd arrive about the time everyone was getting up to pack out of the mountains and return home.

I can't even begin to explain my feelings at that moment—a mixture of anger, frustration, and fear all thrown in a blender and whipped at high speed along with some ice cubes of sweat. All we had to help us was Don's small LED headlight, but I suggested we go ahead and get started, slowly walking down the mountain as he led the way. We hadn't gotten far, though, when I noticed a light approaching. Adam had ridden only a half mile and had come upon our horses grazing along the trail. This was nothing short of a miracle! Horses *always* go back to camp. These horses didn't. We thankfully mounted up.

Then Adam said something unexpected to Don: "Turn off your light. Horses can see in the dark. Trust your horse." Don already knew this. I didn't. The light went out.

It was so dark I couldn't see my hand waving in front of my face. The horses started moving, but I knew any moment that my head was going to be taken off by a low-hanging limb. I expected at some point along the trail that my knee would get caught against a tree, and my hip would be torn out of socket. Sure enough, while I was trying to see in the dark to subdue my fear, a cedar limb brushed my face, scratching my left eye and forcing me to close both eyes and pull my hood down over my face for the remainder of the two-hour ride, all the while holding my Mathews bow in front of me for its own protection.

OUT OF CONTROL

I had known greater heart-thumping fear than this, simply on a scale of one to ten. But I had never known this special *kind* of fear—the fear of being totally out of control of my circumstances. There was absolutely nothing I could do at that moment to alter my destiny. I was at the complete mercy of the horse. And some treacherous rocks on a steep ledge were coming up.

That's when God spoke to me.

I didn't hear any words in my ears, but I heard Him clearly in my heart. I had waited to hear from Him all week, expecting the words to be grand, poetic, book-worthy. Instead, God said four simple words to me: *"I am your horse."*

When I heard these four words—words that I probably would not and *could* not have heard in the stress-filled, fast-paced daily world of the concrete wilderness—I was filled with a peace that consumed my whole body just as the fire had done to the mountainside. I relaxed in the saddle. I flowed with the horse. Trees brushed my legs, pushing them more closely into the animal's side. Branches caressed my head and face, brushing by like fingers stroking hair.

I rode for the next hour and a half with my eyes closed and my head down. I almost went to sleep, in fact, as my horse carried me powerfully along, sticking to a path I couldn't see, carrying me when I had no strength left to carry myself, avoiding the dangers of the woods and the steep drop-off, ready to stomp the skulls of enemy lions or bears or wolves, leading me eventually to the safety of high camp.

WISDOM OUT WEST

I now know why I was supposed to go to Idaho. I needed this experience with God, because my heart was in need of surgery. As I think back on it, before I went to the Idaho mountains my heart was dull and broken and filled with things that were detrimental to my spiritual health:

- Uncertainty regarding my future path in life, and therefore a continual worry about picking out the right path to follow.
- Bitterness and anger over the rejection I had received in previous work situations.

- Disappointment that my energy was growing weaker and weaker and that my creativity seemed to have dried to a trickle.
- Resentment in the material successes of others, while I was working just as hard (or harder!) and not getting the same rewards.
- Delight in the fall of those who had hurt me so deeply. Even though I had prayed for these people, I still felt a tinge of delight when I found out several of them had fallen from their positions of authority and their secret sins had been found out.
- Fear of the unknown darkness in my future, of not knowing exactly where I'd be and what I'd be doing in the days to come. In short, fear of finding myself in a situation over which I had no control.

I was desperately in need of some private time with the Great Physician. I needed to be vividly reminded that I am not a bad person with a bad heart, but that by God's grace I am a good person with a good heart—a person who started out in a loving relationship with God, made in His divine image. I needed to be reminded of my original glory in Christ, a glory I can walk in with head held high.

I needed to believe once again.

God said four words to me in the high country: *"I am your horse."* And my heart will never again be the same.

REFLECT

All of us have experienced the pain of a broken heart. What one thing, more than anything else, has caused YOU to lose heart?

LOOK AT THE BOOK

Consider two verses of Scripture from both the Old and New Testaments that reveal God's promises regarding the heart of man:

I will give you a new heart and put a new spirit within you; I will remove your heart of stone and give you a heart of flesh. I will place My Spirit within you and cause you to follow My statutes and carefully observe My ordinances.—Ezek. 36:26–27

Therefore we do not give up; even though our outer person is being destroyed, our inner person is being renewed day by day. For our momentary light affliction is producing for us an absolutely incomparable eternal weight of glory. So we do not focus on what is seen, but on what is unseen; for what is seen is temporary, but what is unseen is eternal.—2 Cor. 4:16–18

DIG DEEPER

1. What do these two passages say to you?

_____

_____

_____

_____

2. The wonderful twenty-third Psalm contains this line about God: *"He restores my soul"* (v. 3). Turn in your Bible to Psalm 23 and read the entire chapter. Where do you most need His restoration in your life right now?

_____

_____

_____

3. On a scale of 1 to 10, how much time are you spending in God's great outdoors—not just seeking an animal or a fish, but seeking something far more important—an intimate relationship with the One who created the outdoors you love so much? (Circle your answer below.)

1 . . . 2 . . . 3 . . . 4 . . . 5 . . . 6 . . . 7 . . . 8 . . . 9 . . . 10

4. Consider the following verse, also taken from the Psalms: *"He heals the brokenhearted and binds up their wounds"* (Psalm 147:3). What does this verse say to you?

_____

_____

FROM THE HEART

Take an honest look into the deep recesses of your heart. Do you sense the need to spend some time in the mountains or to find a sanctuary for a period of time where you can be removed from the distractions of this world and hear God's voice speaking to you?

Where is this place for you? Or where would you like it to be?

_____

_____

_____

_____

_____

When do you plan to go to this place? (Write the date below.)

_____

POSTSCRIPT

God is the Great Physician, the great heart surgeon, ready to do some open-heart surgery on you.

He can heal your heart. He can remove all of the bitterness, anger, resentment, revenge, hurt, loneliness, and pain. He can replace it with joy, peace, forgiveness, trust, and love.

TROPHIES: RARE MOMENTS

He was big. I mean he was *really* big. I only had to look through my binoculars for two seconds to realize this was the largest deer I'd ever seen. From what I could tell he was at least a ten-pointer. Heavy tined, fat, and full of lust!

I'd made the trip up north to hunt with one of my best buddies. Chuck is a man whose heart holds deep waters. My time with him is pure gold, because I always come back refined from our conversations. I was really looking forward to the time. All of it. The meals, the stories, everything. Hugging my buddy upon arrival, I was thankful for a friend from God.

I arrived at our destination with only one thing on my mind: "How in the world am I going to kill a nice buck in this horrid weather?" Because it wasn't just raining. It was as if God had decided that all the world needed a bath!

I had one thing working for me, though. The rut was in full swing. I'm talking *full swing!* Rain or shine, the antlered boys were fulfilling Bachman Turner Overdrive's prophecy in "takin' care of business and workin' overtime."

So with our GoreTex absolutely soaked from the downpour, we went straight to the woods around 1:30 p.m. The more time you can get in the tree during the rut, the better.

PLAY OR PASS?

I'd been in my tree about an hour when I called up a 120-125 class, huge eight-pointer who had responded to my grunts.

(Field tip: I called this deer in by simply "cold calling"—calling when you don't see anything. If your stand is in a high traffic area, you never know what deer may be around even though you're unaware of it.)

Within sixty seconds of my last grunt, this buck was standing eighteen yards away, ears back, eyes glaring! And boy, was he fat. This deer needed Atkins in the worst way. I got a good, long look at him, and I could tell he would dress around 225 pounds. Neck swollen so big it made his head look small!

I'D BEEN IN MY TREE ABOUT AN HOUR WHEN I CALLED UP A HUGE EIGHT-POINTER.

But I decided to pass. Crazy, I know. A battle raged in my spirit, trying to decide whether or not to draw on this nice animal. And what a hunt that would have been!

Here I was, no more than an hour into my meteorological nightmare, and I was staring down a wall hanger—one that I'd grunted in, no less.

Still, I already had a really nice nine on my wall which was almost identical. I needed discipline in the worst way. But I passed that test, and it would prove to be a defining moment.

Literally.

I climbed down soaked to the core, quietly gathered my gear, and eased out of the woods. I'd be back the next day, well before dawn, to spend the entire daylight hours in that one spot.

FIELDING QUESTIONS

Early the next morning I arrived at my tree. The weather front had moved out, and the day promised to be clearing up and getting colder. The barometer was dropping all day, and it was serving as a plunger to push those whitetails into a frenzy.

Putting on my jacket at an altitude of twenty feet, I heard that all too familiar sound of a deer fast-walking toward me. *You've got to be kidding,* I thought. Sure enough, a nice six-pointer well on his way to maturity walked right under me. My soul churned with warm thoughts from this sign of a good day ahead.

Around 9 a.m. I saw my obese eight-pointer again, a hundred yards away on a dead run through a field, directly into the wind, trailing some does that had come through earlier. No other deer graced my eyes until 1 p.m. when four does came back across the field they had entered hours earlier. They circled behind me and winded me. No problem. I wasn't too bothered. One thing did stick out in my mind, however. Every deer I'd seen on both days had crossed in front of me about a hundred yards out. I knew that

RIGHT THERE IN MY STAND, I SAID, "GOD, WHAT SHOULD I DO? SHOULD I MOVE OR NOT?"

with a 10 mph wind, no deer could hear me grunt if it crossed through that bottleneck of cedars.

The wind would be tricky if I attempted to move. And there was nothing but ten-foot cedars bookending that field, along with some trees that had too many limbs to accommodate my climber (which is why I prefer strap-on tree stands).

So I was faced with a decision. To move or not to move.

My only option would be bow hunting from the ground—something I'd never attempted before. The odds are just so stacked against you. Yet I had made a decision way back in early bow season that this year I would attempt some really off-the-wall tactics. Do some stuff I normally wouldn't.

So I prayed about it. Right there in my stand twenty feet above the earth, I had a short talk with my Father above. "God, what should I do? Should I move or not?"

Friend, I realize that you don't know me, but trust me when I say to you that over the next two minutes, I began to feel a confirmation in my spirit that simply said, "You need to move." That was at 3:40 p.m. And by 4 p.m. my feet were on *terra firma*.

NOW OR NEVER

As I assembled my tree stand—now just a liability to carry back to the truck—what did I encounter but a loud snort! A deer shot away from me at only sixty yards! I never even saw its head, which caused me to apply my own stock rule about busting deer: any one I spook by accident must be a doe! (This helps the ego.) Oddly enough, though, I wasn't that rattled. I still felt good about moving.

I continued on about seventy-five yards toward the bottleneck that connected the two fields. Ten minutes later, six does came right up behind me and crossed the field where every other deer had headed. I knew I was at ground zero, and I needed to stay.

Five minutes later, the twenty-sixth deer of the day—a small seven-pointer—trotted by at 150 yards to my left.

It was now 4:15 p.m. I prayed again. This time, though, it wasn't about moving. "God, barring some miracle over the next hour, I'm going to need a special dose of grace tomorrow."

4:30 p.m. That's when he stepped out. At 200 yards. And he was big. I mean he was *really* big. Through my glasses he looked like a big ten or better.

Nose to the ground, he was all business, crossing the fence from an adjacent farm. Sweeping for does, he was fast-walking the field edge directly toward me . . . and quickly closing the gap! For a few minutes he crossed over into a small one-acre finger of woods along the fence line. I thought he was going over into the next field.

That's it, I thought. *I'm cutting him off. I'm moving.* I was either going to score or fail miserably. No in-betweens.

I had taken only five steps when I glanced back to the field. There he was. All he'd done was step into that sliver of woods to scent-check it.

Wow. He was trotting closer to me now. Probably 150 yards away. I got on my face, prostrate. Nose to the ground, I Marine-crawled back to my hideout on the field edge. Both time and the buck were moving faster than I was. He was getting closer, and I needed time to set up.

I pulled my quiver off my bow, ran an arrow through my Whisker Biscuit, and leaned back on my leg.

HEART RACE

At a hundred yards, he was directly to my right, about seventy yards from the tree line I was bunkered in. Set up in the shadows of a cedar tree, I grunted. He stopped with militant force. He knew what he'd heard. I grunted again, and the unexpected happened. Never before had I seen this.

He opened his mouth as wide as he could, tongue hanging down like a panting dog after a long run, and bellowed a wicked guttural grunt that lasted three full seconds. He then sprinted right at me.

Man! My heart is racing at this very moment as I write this, my hands literally shaking on the keyboard. No joke. I can see it like it was ten minutes ago.

On a dead run at me, he had nothing but pure love on his mind. My problem was that I couldn't get my release attached to the string! (I shoot a Scott rope release.) It wasn't that I was rattled by him. Seriously, I wasn't. I was as calm as ever. But my rope release was bent back a little, and I couldn't get it to connect.

I took my eyes off him and slowly checked my nock for a tight fit. I then put my release on the string and gave it tension.

AT FIFTEEN YARDS, I GRUNTED. HE STOPPED. WE WERE EYEBALL TO EYEBALL.

Just fifty yards away now, he was still on a trot, but a persimmon tree began obscuring my field of vision. I couldn't see him. He couldn't see me. I drew quick.

At twenty-five yards I had a shot, but he was committed to continue, so I let him.

At fifteen yards I grunted and he stopped. We were eyeball to eyeball. The arrow took flight. Honed in, target acquired.

Thump.

He whirled around, and I saw my carbon beauty fly out fully intact. The broadhead had answered my call.

MAN, OH, MAN!

As the midwestern sun set over the freshly cut bean field showing signs of green life, my buck ran directly away from me and stopped at a hundred yards in the middle of the arena. Standing there for ten seconds or so, he was gathering the wind and assessing the situation.

Timber! Not another step.

Rising to my feet, I imitated the quarterback hero of my youth, Joe Montana. Like the 49er giant who had just thrown a game-winning TD pass to Dwight Clark, I rose with both hands to the sky, fists clinched. But in letting out a hunter's *yawp*, I began to panic. With adrenaline shooting through my veins faster than ever, the gravity of what had just occurred pressed its full weight into my mind. I'd just shot a massive trophy whitetail with a bow from fifteen yards while hunting on the ground.

No way. *No way!* He was down—and not even attempting to move!

The next seventy-five minutes can only be described as cruel and unusual punishment. Slow torture. I knew he was dead. I had an hour of daylight left. But there was no way I was going out to claim my prize. Not yet.

I sat down. I rehearsed all that I knew to be true: Don't panic. Don't do anything stupid. Let him lay. Find something to do. So I packed up my gear.

That took about three minutes.

Great. Now what?

I then forced myself to return to my rendezvous point with Chuck. That would mean a fifteen minute walk. At least.

Over the next hour I waited for my brother to arrive. I was dying inside. But walking up to me, Chuck knew there was no need to ask. "Man, I got him!" I said.

"Did you really?" Chuck said. "What is he?"

"A big ten. At least!" I said.

We both went out to the field's epicenter, and there he was. No movement. He'd given up the ghost!

"Wait!" I said. "He's not a ten!" I counted seven on the first side. I counted seven on the other.

"You've got to be kidding me!" A fourteen-point monster with a double main beam.

"Jason Cruise, what have you done?" my buddy shouted. "Now, that's a buck!"

It took me a full week to gather my thoughts over what had happened to me on that beautifully crafted November evening. In fact, this is the first time I've really put words to it formally. I may go the rest of my life and never see a deer that large again.

Fine by me. I've been blessed. I was blessed before then, and now I'm just experiencing grace!

There's no doubt in my mind God designed that hunt for me. *Just for me!* He wanted that deer for me because He knew it would bring me joy. And it did!

REFLECT

What's the largest set of antlers you've seen in the wild? Describe your encounter in a short paragraph.

_____

_____

_____

_____

_____

_____

_____

_____

_____

_____

_____

LOOK AT THE BOOK

A thief comes only to steal and to kill and to destroy. I have come that they may have life and have it in abundance.—John 10:10

Jesus told us He came to give us life. The full life. But one thing I've learned about life in Christ is that we have no idea just how much Satan hates us. He hates everything about us because we embody God's image and are inhabited by His Spirit. Satan hates that.

He realizes, for example, that he can't steal your soul. I mean, once you're in Christ, you're in. To stay! But that doesn't stop Satan from being a thief. And I believe the number one thing he loves to steal from believers is joy. He gets prime satisfaction from making us miserable.

Yet even with Satan actively working against us, joy is a choice we make. It's a state of the soul. It's our responsibility.

We all learn over time that when we look for happiness in other people, or in our job, or in our hobbies, we never find it. That's because happiness is not the same as joy. Happiness has nothing to do with what is "happening." Happiness is momentary. It's like finding a ten-dollar bill in a parking lot.

God wants to give you joy. He's already said that. *"Take delight in the Lord, and He will give you your heart's desires"* (Ps. 37:4). God wants to give you trophy moments, but one thing's for sure: you can't see trophy moments when you're blinded by resentment and pain. It's up to you to let joy come back to you. So if your heart has no song, you need to dig deep and find out why. What did you do to let your joy leave and stay gone?

I can't tell you why God let me take that trophy buck. I don't deserve that. I really don't. Yet it happened, and God took pleasure from my pleasure!

He's just that kind of Father.

DIG DEEPER

What have you learned about the heart of God that can help you get that joy back?

When do you find that your joy is most compromised—or perhaps missing altogether?

FROM THE HEART

Think of someone you know (maybe several someones) who are running short in the joy department. You can put them on your prayer list, for sure, but how else might God want to use you to help them rekindle His joy in their lives?

_____

_____

_____

_____

_____

_____

POSTSCRIPT

One thing I didn't tell you was that my trip up north only happened because I had to cancel an elk hunting trip out west. I desperately wanted to go but I just wasn't able. Yet I chose to let that frustration go, and it wasn't easy.

I'm so glad God let me see His goodness during this hunt, because it taught me something more about His character. He loves to see me smile. He loves to see me succeed. He had a trophy moment waiting for me up north—not out west!

LATE SEASON

Forgetting what is behind and reaching forward to what is ahead, I pursue as my goal the prize promised by God's heavenly call in Christ Jesus.

Philippians 3:13–14

You're tired. Maybe even frustrated. But late season can be some of the greatest hunting you'll ever do—if you'll stay with it. That's what makes you different. You're not just a fair weather hunter. You know that the late season is characterized by one foremost strategy: perseverance. You won't put your tag on him from the comforts of your couch. If it's going to happen, you've got to get out there, engage the weather, bear down, and get it done.

STAY IN IT

You've been there. It's late in the season, and you've yet to fill your tag with the buck you wanted. You know what it feels like to go through the gauntlet of late season. Just the sound of the words—*late season*—emit this eerie smell of emotion, don't they? The "late" feeling makes you feel like you're under intense pressure to deliver.

Let me take you way back—about 16 years—to a hunt where I became enlightened to the power of the late season.

Time: December
Place: Tennessee farmland
Set Up: My trusty stand site, tucked away on the back corner of the property

It was cold and the sun was going down—the last day of the second black powder season, which usually lands close to mid-December. I had yet to see a deer, which came as no surprise, given that it was well past the rut and the big fellas were regrouping their energy to make it through the winter.

I had thirty minutes before sundown.

Figuring that it was do or die, I decided to *do!* Perhaps taking the fight to the deer would be better than seeing if they brought it to me which, from my current perspective, seemed a very slim possibility.

GETTING LATER ALL THE TIME

I climbed down in a hurry, gathered my gear, and headed down a logging road toward a small green field that rested just over the ridge from my stand. It was no more than three acres, but it did hold clover, which is a super late-season food source.

As I arrived within sight of the field, I dropped to a bent-over walk because I knew I had a chance of being seen if there were any deer in that field. Crawling the last thirty yards to the edge where the tree line gave way to the sage grass, I saw movement. Raising my binoculars, I laid eyes on the most beautiful gift a hunter can receive . . . a nice set of antlers late in the season.

There he was. A really nice eight-pointer just feeding his way into the evening, gathering all the clover he could stomach.

I had maybe ten minutes of shooting light left. It was dead silent.

You know how it is—one of those late winter days with absolutely no wind, no clouds, and only a bright blue sky giving way to the amber sunset.

As if he were on a retractable string, the buck raised his head and walked quickly, right in my direction, closing the gap now to about seventy-five yards. Wow! I really was going to get a shot. I couldn't believe how quickly things were changing in my favor.

Back then I owned what was the first in the arena of in-line muzzleloaders. It misfired a little less often than more traditional guns, but by today's standards you wouldn't even hunt with it! I was quite accurate with it, though, and I felt good about this shot in particular.

Hammer back, I squeezed. Next came that moment any black-powder hunter experiences—that love-hate window of three seconds it takes for the smoke to clear from around your face. It's not so bad in some conditions, but when the humidity is mixed with just the right temperature, it can be pure torture.

That's what it was like on this day.

Through the evaporating smoke, I could see my buck on the ground. The deed was done. My season, as well as the condition of my heart, had just changed from ashes to glory.

MY SEASON HAD JUST CHANGED FROM ASHES TO GLORY.

He was no monster buck but, boy, was he worth bragging to my buddies over! To this day, his antlers serve as my set of rattling horns. At this very moment they hang on a cord over a nail piercing the outside of my hunting closet.

STAY IN IT

Where I live, there's a morning show on the radio during drive time hosted by a couple of good ol' boys named Rick and Bubba. They believe in the Lord Jesus Christ, and yet they're not stuffy about it. They're my kind of guys. They don't take themselves too seriously and seem to find humor in the everyday events of this seemingly chaotic world.

I've been in the loop of their listening audience for many years now. And being a longtime fan, I've retained many of the code words they use in their secret vocabulary when they want to convey meaning in a short amount of time.

"Big Red," for example, is code for Satan and his deceptive schemes.

"For the love" is code for "Hey, would you give me a break?"

Yet perhaps my favorite Rick and Bubba turn-of-phrase is this one: "Stay in it!" This, of course, carries the idea of someone staying in the game when it gets tough. If my Rick and Bubba history is accurate, this line originated from rednecks who would spin their tires while laying down some rubber. Rick states that when someone would get to flooring the gas pedal, he and his cronies would yell, "Stay in it!"

I like this phrase for a number of reasons, mainly because it's so versatile. Believe it or not, I even use this little vocabulary triplet when I'm about to pull the trigger. Growing up in the golf world, I know the importance of simple mental reminders when you get into pressure situations. So when I ease the safety into "go" position, the last thing I tell myself is, "Stay in it!" It's my reminder to myself: *Follow through and stay down on the shot!*

THE DIFFERENCE HOPE MAKES

Late season hunting has everything to do with staying in it, because it's built around one simple idea—hope. Never underestimate the power of hope, in hunting or in life.

Hope gets me out of bed on mornings when it's 10 degrees. Hope keeps me in the woods when the clouds dump water on my Gore-Tex. Hope is what allowed me to take that December buck sixteen years ago.

There's a difference between me and most hunters. I'm not talking in terms of talent. There are many hunters out there who are just simply better at harvesting larger bucks on a much larger frequency than, say, a guy like me.

LATE SEASON HUNTING IS BUILT AROUND ONE SIMPLE IDEA—HOPE.

But I believe what separates me from many in my fraternity of outdoorsmen is simple: persistence and hope. What I lack in talent, I make up for in persistence.

When most guys aren't in the field, I will be. Rain, cold winds, even sporting a late season and empty tag, I'll be there. And, man, has that character trait paid off for me so many times.

There's an old cliché that says, "Ninety percent of success is showing up." This is a core truth I live by. You know as well as I do that so often hunting comes down to being in the right place at the right time. Yes, you have to know where that right place is located. But you can't cash in on the moment if you're not there!

THE LATE SEASON ADVANTAGE

Hunting late season can be life-changing. There's a lot going for you if you think about it. The main advantage you have, in my opinion, is a decreasing amount of hunting pressure. Fewer shots are ringing through the air.

HUNTING SO OFTEN COMES DOWN TO BEING IN THE RIGHT PLACE AT THE RIGHT TIME.

As a rule, most hunters are what I call token hunters. They give a token effort toward their buck or bull. They do hunt hard, but they're more closely related to microwaves than crock pots. They heat up fast and hunt hard until conditions get tough and game becomes scarce. Then they cool down.

Ah, but the glory of the crock pot! Longer to warm up, but it heats thoroughly and lasts all day. When you hunt long into the year, hunting just as hard as the opening day, you'll eventually reap the harvest of what you've sowed.

REFLECT

1. List your favorite late season gear, the stuff you won't leave home without.

_____

_____

_____

_____

2. What are some spiritual tools you shouldn't leave home without, as well?

_____

_____

_____

_____

LOOK AT THE BOOK

Not that I have already obtained all this, or have already been made perfect, but I press on to take hold of that for which Christ Jesus took hold of me. Brothers, I do not consider myself yet to have taken hold of it. But one thing I do: Forgetting what is behind and straining toward what is ahead, I press on toward the goal to win the prize for which God has called me heavenward in Christ Jesus.
—Philippians 3:12–14 NIV

If there's one thing that life in Christ has taught me, it's this—a believer plays to the rules of a different game. Most of the people in this world live off what some call luck or good breaks, hoping things go their way. Nothing could be further from the truth, however, when it comes to living under the power of God.

To be in Christ means that you don't operate with the same rule book the rest of the world plays by.

- While many rely on shallow horoscopes, you rely on the very Word of God.
- While many turn to ruthlessness for their job security, you turn to the power of God.
- While many count on a year-end bonus, you count on being blessed by God.
- You operate by the rules of a different game, and you get different results.

Paul knew this. He was a man who knew what it meant to have the odds stacked against him. He knew what it meant to be without money. He knew what it meant to be fed and what it meant to be hungry. He knew what it meant to be accepted, and he knew what it meant to be lonely from being rejected . . . which makes his statement from Philippians 3 across the page even more incredible.

Call it what you will, persistence is based on an axiom of truth straight from the heart of God: "Press on!" And what gives us the ability to press on? Hope. Not wishful thinking, not candyland dreaming. The hope we have as believers is based on reality—the reality that Jesus Christ purchased our freedom from sin on the cross. And His freedom carries with it some amazingly eternal perks—namely, hope.

Our hope is built on the fact that Jesus beat death through the Resurrection.

DIG DEEPER

Take a minute right now and tell God that you'll follow Him through the rough country because you know He's leading you.

FROM THE HEART

I want you to read this very carefully from here on. I realize that the cross is the central figure of Christianity. Yet from what I gather in studying it, the cross as the central theme came along a few centuries after Jesus' ascension. Some theologians say that it wasn't until around 300 AD that the cross became the icon of recognition for Christians.

Care to know what the icon was before that? *An open grave!*

Okay, I want you to read even *more* carefully now so you don't misunderstand me. I'm not saying that the cross shouldn't be our central figure. What I am saying is that on the day Jesus died on a cross, two other men died right beside Him in the same way. In fact, thousands of people were crucified on Roman crosses. *But only One came out of the grave never to die again!*

And that's hope. Hope to "press on."

POSTSCRIPT

No matter where your season of life is right now, realize that if you're following the path of Christ, you have Someone who has gone before you into the rugged country ahead. Your life is not some random journey that has no guaranteed end. You have God's promise that His power will guide you through the High Country of your life.

PAYING ATTENTION
TO DETAILS

Day six. I sat elevated fifteen feet above the frozen ground of the Boreal Forest in northern Saskatchewan, Canada. My bow was hanging from a limb just to my left. The thermometer registered 10 degrees Fahrenheit. It was cold!

I was layered with all the warm clothing I had brought on the trip, and then had to squeeze into an orange jumpsuit that made me look like the Pillsbury Doughboy at a Texas Longhorn or Tennessee Volunteers game. Such is the law in Saskatchewan even during bow season.

A few does and small bucks came through from time to time, but I had yet to see a shooter buck in five days. The key in Saskatchewan is persistence. If you stay out there long enough, you'll see a big buck. I'm talking 300 pounds on the hoof, sporting thick, gnarly racks with dark bases. Boone and Crocket bucks are frequently harvested in Saskatchewan, including the world record Hanson buck.

The thought of such a big buck showing up under my bow stand kept me sitting minute after cold minute during the twelve-hour days. My cameraman Don Belles was right there with me, elevated a few feet above me.

THE LITTLE THINGS

Don is a seasoned bow hunter, one of the best outdoorsmen I know. He is notorious for paying attention to the details. For example, a heavy sleet swept through the treetops for half an hour as we sat. Afterwards, Don leaned down and whispered, "Jimmy, check your peep sight."

"I did when we got here," I replied.

"Check it again," Don encouraged. I slowly stood up, drew my bow, looked into my peep, and saw nothing but frozen particles of ice. If the biggest buck in the world had walked in and stood broadside, I wouldn't have had a chance at him. I couldn't see anything! I blew hot breath through the peep and cleared it out.

Lesson learned. Small details such as this one can make or break a successful hunt.

For example, mid-afternoon on the final day I decided to draw my bow and take a shot at a rotten stump about twenty yards away. I wanted to make sure my bow wasn't frozen up from the cold (and to limber up my stiff muscles).

After the shot, I reached to retrieve another

arrow from the quiver only to find that my arrows were frozen solid in there. I couldn't get a second one out until I had breathed on the quiver for about two solid minutes. Once again, I learned a valuable lesson about hunting in extreme conditions. I took out a Hot Hands pack, shook it a few times to ignite it, then stuffed it in the middle of my arrows within the quiver. The heat warmed the carbon shafts enough to free them from the frozen precipitation.

I also noticed that when I drew back to take the practice shot, the pull-string tightening my fleece head net was coming in contact with my bowstring when I settled into my anchor point. It was just enough to throw off my shot by a few inches, or at least to make additional noise when I took the shot. So I tucked the pull-string under the collar of my jacket.

Having taken care of all of these small details, I felt that I was totally ready for any scenario that might play out if a big buck came in. Little did I know that I would find out differently in a couple of hours.

THE SLIGHTEST SOUND

With two hours of daylight left on the final day, I sensed something approaching in a thicket to my left. "Deer," I whispered to Don through the lapel mic attached to my jacket.

It didn't take long for both of us to see what was now only forty yards away and moving in our direction. A huge nine-point buck was cautiously working his way in, on line to step out of the thicket at eighteen yards.

I quietly drew my bow, waiting on the buck to emerge. This was going to be a perfect way to end the hunt!

And that's when it happened. Don did nothing more than lift the camera from his lap to his shoulder to record the action. But as he did, his feet shifted only slightly on the aluminum stand. A metallic pop stopped the deer in his tracks, and within a couple of seconds the big buck was bolting away and out of sight. Don's boots had frozen to the stand, and the metallic pop was the sound of them breaking free.

This could have been prevented if only we had thought to cover the bottom of the stand with a sheet, some rubber, or even a blanket. But we went home to Nashville without taking one shot at a Saskatchewan buck.

Once again, lesson learned. Details matter.

INFIELDING

The same is true for our life on earth.

If you're like me, I'm sure you can think of an event in your own life where you did just about everything perfectly, but because of one small oversight the whole thing ended up as a failure.

Maybe it was a business deal that flew south at the last moment, or an invention that was going to bankroll your retirement, but someone else beat you to the patent. It might have been something as huge as your marriage, or a relationship with your son or daughter. Even worse, it could have been a rupture in your spiritual journey that's had a domino effect on your relationship with God and the church.

Like I said, details matter. This is most true when it comes to obeying all of God's commands. Don't fool yourself into thinking you can be a good person and obey most of God's commands while refusing to obey just one—and still be in a good relationship with Him.

I've seen this with my own eyes. I know of individuals who call themselves Christians, do many good things, and even go to church on a weekly basis. Yet they choose to live in an adulterous situation with someone they're not married to. Jesus addressed such people in Matthew 7:22–23 when he reported:

"On that day many will say to Me, 'Lord, Lord, didn't we prophesy in Your name, drive out demons in Your name, and do many miracles in Your name?' Then I will announce to them, 'I never knew you. Depart from Me, you lawbreakers!'"

WHEN THINGS SEEM TO BE GOING WELL, IT'S WHEN I'M PAYING ATTENTION TO THE DETAILS.

We have to pay attention to every detail of God's Word.

Please understand that I'm not always successful at practicing what I preach. Sometimes I don't even come close to hitting the target. Occasionally I'm off center by two rings. But more and more I am beginning to hit the bull's-eye. It's a spiritual growth process of maturing in my walk with Christ. I've noticed that when things seem to be going well for me in my spiritual journey, it's when I'm paying special attention to the details of what really matters in my day-to-day life.

DIFFERENCE MAKERS

Based on what I've learned during my adventure with God, here are some suggestions regarding how you can pay attention to the details that really matter in your spiritual life:

• *Read*. Make sure you're feeding yourself a meal from God's Word every day by reading something in the Bible. Your spiritual body needs nourishment just as much as your physical body does. After all, Jesus called himself the "bread of life" (John 6:35) and said that He offers "living water" (John 4:10; 7:37–38).

• *Dig*. If spending time in the Word is a constant struggle for you, choose a translation of the Bible you can easily understand, rather than using an outdated version that bogs you down in archaic language and is hard to comprehend.

• *Pray*. Respond to God about what you're reading. Talk with Him just as you would a hunting companion. Respect Him as a Guide. Trust Him. But don't be so scared of Him that you avoid Him. Ask Him questions. Let Him know your weaknesses. Ask for His help. Thank Him. Love Him. This is what prayer's all about.

• *Worship*. Don't become so busy with your daily tasks, including trying to harvest a wild animal or catch a trophy fish, that you overlook the fingerprints of God. They're everywhere!

Take time to enjoy a sunset. Try to distinguish the various sounds of life as they penetrate your ears. Stop to watch a colony of ants as they work together. Look deeply into a baby's eyes. Watch children at play. Count the colors in the fall leaves. Join with nature in praising God for His creation (see Ps. 19:1–4).

• *Stay pure.* Try to see people for who they really are—creatures made in the image of God. Rather than looking at a beautiful woman as an object of sexual desire, try to see her as a child of God. Realize that no matter her age or appearance, she is someone's daughter. Treat her as you'd want other men to treat your own daughter or even your wife.

• *Care.* Take a moment to do something nice for someone. Make daily deposits into the bank of relationships with those you love the most. The more of these you make, the more "interest" will be paid to you by those people. A daily deposit is something as simple as taking out the trash without being asked, or making the bed when it's someone else's assignment. You might even try writing a simple note such as "I think you're awesome" or "I love you," and slipping it into your child's wallet or purse while they're not looking. Stop and pick some wildflowers for your wife and surprise her even when it's not your anniversary. These daily deposits don't take much effort, but they pay great dividends!

• *Serve.* Practice serving people you don't know well. Give a bottle of cold water to the trash man. Leave a small Christmas present for the mail carrier. Let someone else go ahead of you in traffic. Treat all people in such a way that it reminds them they're special. When the cashier is rude to you, don't retaliate. Give that person the benefit of the doubt that they could be having a very bad day. Try to make it better by speaking kind words in return.

• *Be smart.* Admit your weaknesses and avoid placing yourself into situations where you may fail. If you're a recovering alcoholic, stay away from bars. If you have a problem with pornography, have a friend program your Internet and your cable television with locks that will prevent you from visiting those sites. If you're prone to discipline your children in anger, build in a one-hour "safe zone" that will give you time to calm down before you continue the disciplining. If you hunt with buddies who consistently violate game laws, get some new hunting buddies!

• *Get into church.* Seek one out in your area that believes in the power of the Word of God and bases everything they do on what God says to do. Don't settle for a church that allows you to slip in the door, sit on the back pew, and never become involved in the daily life of being the body of Christ. Search for a place that'll hold you accountable to pulling your part of the load. Become involved!

• *Speak softly.* Check your words, because they carry great power that can cause either a positive or harmful effect. Get control of negative thoughts, and don't set them free to do their damage when you speak them. This is especially true if you have children. Your words shape them more than you know. If you tell them they're stupid, don't be surprised when they do stupid things. If you tell them they're the most incredible children you've ever seen, don't be surprised when they end up doing incredible things that will boggle your mind. Refuse to contribute to the chaos of the world by speaking negative words.

LAWS OF THE LATE SEASON

These are just a few of the details of the Christian life that are borne out in God's Word, in common sense, and in experience. I'm sure you can think of others. Bottom line: if we're going to be followers of Jesus, we must learn to pay attention to the details of daily living.

Remember the lessons I learned on the bow hunt in Saskatchewan. Also, think about your own hunting experiences. Late season hunts are often either successful or blown based on small details. Hunters who haven't yet filled their tag and are forced to hunt later in the year often get sloppy.

Never get lax in remembering that when you're in the outdoors, you're on the animal's turf. You have to outsmart a creature that is naturally on the defensive already and has been hunted for several weeks or months. The weather is tougher, the terrain is more open with the leaves being gone, and the air currents carry scent further, alerting animals to your presence.

What do you do? You pay attention to the small details and stack the deck in your favor. You take it to the next level.

And that's exactly what God is inviting you to do in your spiritual walk with Him. The best news of all is that He is willing to empower you to do these things, to walk the trail with you. He is volunteering to serve as your Guide who stands ready to help you.

Will you let Him?

REFLECT

1. Have you ever had a hunt blown because you didn't pay attention to a small detail? If so, record your experience in the Field Journal below.

_____

_____

_____

_____

2. Now think of a time when you overlooked a detail in your spiritual life and it ended up causing you to "miss the mark" (the definition of sin). What detail did you overlook that brought about this outcome?

_____

_____

_____

_____

_____

LOOK AT THE BOOK

Work out your own salvation with fear and trembling.
—Philippians 2:12

Paul wrote these words in his letter to the church at Philippi during the first century AD. Much discussion has taken place about this statement in the centuries since then. Some have concluded that Paul was saying we must work hard in order to merit salvation from God. In other words, good works lead to grace from God.

Let's think through this for a minute, though. If my salvation is based on the quality and quantity of good works I accomplish, I don't think I'll ever make it. I don't have either the ability or the energy to do enough good works to earn the grace of God. It is far more valuable and precious than anything I can generate by what I do.

If I believe that my good works open up the fountain of God's grace in my life, I will likely live a life of anxiety and guilt. I will never be fully satisfied that I'm saved because I'll always feel that I have to do more.

So for anyone who believes that works lead to grace—and therefore to salvation—an adjustment needs to be made. Don't throw the baby out with the bath water, just reverse the rhythm:

Works don't lead to grace.
Grace leads to works.

When you understand grace as a free gift from God you can't possibly earn, it frees you up to receive the gift and be overwhelmed by God's generosity. Do you have any part in it? Yes, you choose to receive it. But that's it. You can't earn it and you certainly don't deserve it. But the good news of the gospel is that you get it anyway because He loves you so much!

When you realize this and can live your life from a sense of wonder and amazement at how good God is to you, you'll be motivated to serve Him with all of your heart and body. You'll *want* to please Him with good works. You'll *want* to honor Him in every way you possible can.

Instead of going through life with a religious "got to" mentality, you can go through life with a "get to" mentality. Instead of just seeing the Bible as a "law book," you can see it as a "love book." What a difference!

DIG DEEPER

1. So what does Paul mean when he says, *"Work out your own salvation with fear and trembling"*? (Circle the answer that best answers this question in your own mind.)

- Do good deeds for God so He'll love me more, maybe even enough to save me.

- Use my fear of God's wrath to motivate me and spur me along to do good works.

- Go about doing good works from the base camp of my salvation, knowing that I serve the awesome and powerful Creator of the universe with whom I have a mind-boggling relationship.

2. The context of a verse is very important. Read all of Philippians 2:12–13: *"So then, my dear friends, just as you have always obeyed, not only in my presence, but now even more in my absence, work out your own salvation with fear and trembling. For it is God who is working in you, enabling you both to will and to act for His good purpose."*

Did you catch that last phrase? *"For it is God who is working in you."* When you become a follower of God, His Spirit lives in you. He has already proven His love for you by sending His only Son to die on a cross for your sins. Now He is willing to dwell within you and walk with you step by step through life's journey.

That's why Paul, writing to another group of Christians in the region of Galatia, said, *"If we live by the Spirit, we must also follow the Spirit"* (Galatians 5:25). When we do this, we bear the *"fruit of the Spirit . . . love, joy, peace, patience, kindness, goodness, faith, gentleness, self-control"* (Galatians 5:22–23). In other words, we pay attention to the details!

3. As we live within this rhythm with God, we express our love to Him by what we do. Jesus Himself said, *"If you love Me, you will keep My commandments"* (John 14:15). In other words, we have the privilege of expressing our love for the One who has saved us from our sins by doing good works for Him. It's a "get to," not a "got to." Our paying attention to the details is motivated by love, not by law. Remember, nothing is impossible

with God. If you're His follower, He works great power within you. You can join the apostle Paul in believing, *"I am able to do all things through Him who strengthens me"* (Phil. 4:13).

FROM THE HEART

1. Jimmy provided a checklist of suggested details in this chapter you might pay close attention to as you express your love to God on a daily basis. Review this list and pick out the one or two details you need to focus on the most at this time in your life.

1 _____
2 _____

2. What's your plan of action over the next thirty days to implement these details into your daily walk with God? (Be specific.)

_____
_____
_____
_____

POSTSCRIPT

Remember, nothing is impossible with God. If you are His follower, He works a great power within you. You can join the apostle Paul in believing, "I am able to do all things through Him who strengthens me" (Phil. 4:13).

WHAT DEFINES A
SUCCESSFUL SEASON?

Daylight was minutes away. And as the gray clouds fought a losing battle with the rising sun, I couldn't wait to see what was ahead of me. It was my first trip into the high country. God was waking up the earth around me, and I was speechless.

Stepping out of the truck to rearrange the gear in my pack, my buddy Rich began to whistle at me through the rear window. Looking his direction, I saw he had his glasses up and focused high upon a canyon rim. *Already in it!*

Gripping my optics quickly, my eyes connected for the first time in my life with mule deer—the ghosts of North America. My first trip to the high country, and I had decided to take on what is arguably the hardest hunt on the continent—a muley buck.

As a young hunter growing up in Tennessee, I tend to have this mystical reverence for the frontier states. Hunting out west seems so primal. Untouched. And this hunt had me pumped with excitement. I'm not going to play around like I had an aw-shucks attitude about it. Just like every time I go out, I was in hot pursuit of a nice rack.

From what we could tell, there were at least five muley ladies traversing the ridgeline through the morning twilight. The silence was deafening. It's a common emotion I feel every time I go out west. You can hear the silence. Wide open spaces have their own way of talking without saying a word.

But I couldn't wait to stir things up a little.

HIDE AND SEEK

We moved up the canyon rim only to find that they were gone. Nowhere to be found. True to form, the ghosts had vanished. Whitetails, elk, and muleys don't survive by being stupid.

I did have an option, though. I had a buck tag, as well as a tag for cow elk. Willing to take both, I'd settle for either—but I really wanted to call both my wife *and* my taxidermist at the end of this hunt! Time would tell.

We hunted hard, man. I mean hard. Probably walked five miles or more over some rough country. That's when Rich pointed me toward a fixed point and told me to spot and stalk my way for about the next two hours. We made plans to meet up again later, along the canyon line.

Forty minutes into my route, I spotted movement. Lots of it. Dropping to a knee, I had a decent view between the junipers surrounding me like loose clouds. *Yeah! Pronghorn!* A very nice buck was among them, too, and they had no idea I was in their world. The largest buck, in fact, was a Boone & Crockett animal.

But given that I was tagless, I simply admired his beauty for the next ten minutes as the crowd moved along on its way.

All day on a massive ranch, and I didn't lay eyes on another deer. I was learning some fast lessons about big muleys. All the stories I'd read were proving to be true; it's a hard, hard hunt and you've just got to be patient. They have so many places to hide, so many ways they can blend in. And on virtually every rim line they have the advantage of sight, sound, and (most certainly) smell. They can pick you off without you ever knowing they existed.

AN UNEXPECTED FIND

The next morning I sat along a creek bottom with a fairly good line of sight. An hour later I was glassing two huge does just working for food. Ten minutes behind them was a mack-daddy of a coyote. He, too, was working for food.

It reminded me of the danger that's always present in the high country. Everything that lives there has one goal—survival. And they all do it very well.

It reminded me, too, that I must be aware at all times. This was cougar country. Mountain lions hunt back! Just days before, a lady had shot a mountain lion she just happened to see as she looked over her shoulder. Her attacker had been stalking her a mere hundred yards away. Sobering.

Hunting through the noon hour, I drove over to another part of the ranch. I was in the middle of nowhere and loving it. A couple of miles in the distance I could see the Three Sisters. What impressive mountains they are!

Then, only a half mile from the truck, I struck gold. Stopping dead in my tracks I was afraid to move. I couldn't believe my eyes. The thought *"Incredible!"* crossed my mind. My heart raced and a smile came across my face.

In Tennessee we call an eight-pointer an eight-pointer. But out west it would be a 4 x 4, or a four-point. I didn't need my binoculars to tell me, however, that this was at least a five-point.

Or at least he *had* been.

Yes, I'd stumbled upon my first ever antler shed. In the South, antlers don't last long after they leave a buck. Between the leaves, rot, mildew, and squirrels, antlers are a rare find unless you really want to spend time during the first few weeks of the shed.

As crazy as it may sound, I knew at that moment my hunt was a success. A high, tall shed of a buck. My first one. And I found it on my first hunt in the high country. Only two hours later I'd

EVERYTHING THAT LIVES THERE HAS ONE GOAL— SURVIVAL! AND THEY ALL DO IT VERY WELL.

find another really nice shed from a bull elk. A five-point.

Still yet to see antlers intact and on the head of a buck, though, I was looking forward to the next day . . . my last day.

SHORT ON TIME

The following morning we attempted a different hunt. Though the ranch never sees too much pressure to begin with, there had been a family hunting a few days prior to my arrival. So we decided to hunt what equated to probably 5,000 acres on the very front part of the ranch. Untouched country. Perhaps it would prove to house the buck we'd been looking for.

A ranch hand had seen several nice bucks a few weeks prior. One in particular was said to be a hoss.

That morning my hunt was sweetened by a third shed, another five-point with heavy mass. Moving ahead I rested on a canyon rim and watched three does move gracefully across the land. A deep canyon creek swung from my right while rolling prairie bordered my left.

Like something out of a Western, my mind drifted back 150 years. I could just see a cowboy moving along the land, rugged and independent. The only thing he could depend on was the grit in his gut and a good horse. I could see a family making their way down that endless pass that housed the open, grassy creek bed as they made their way through Oregon.

The sun was high overhead now. I only had

about five hours left to connect with my buck. We navigated our way toward the end of the ranch to look for an ounce of hope to finish the hunt. Rich decided to go look around the upside of the next canyon and told me to stay put and glass the areas ahead.

Five minutes later, in what was to be a forty-five minute separation, I saw him walking toward me. Something was up. He'd found elk, and I had a cow tag. With only four hours to go, this was my opportunity to avoid being skunked.

LONG SHOT

The wind in our face, with the herd on the adjacent canyon line, we couldn't have created a better environment to get a shot. Placing tall junipers in their line of sight, we crawled up to our closest shooting point.

The only problem: it was a 300-yard shot. The herd was slowly feeding away from us, and we simply did not have the luxury of coming up behind them without the wind blowing our cover.

It was here or nowhere.

I crawled up into a low-lying juniper which God must have created just in case a guy ever needed to shoot an elk! The limbs set up perfectly. I stretched out my 7 Mag over its thick bark and gazed through my scope. Amazing. Every elk filled my lens completely. The size of these animals was beyond belief.

Just left of the cow I was homing in on, I noticed something out of place. I saw an ear flicker. Increasing the zoom on my scope, I laid eyes on the first bull I'd ever seen. He was a 5 x 5, bedded down under a thick tree. Magnificent. What I wouldn't have paid right there, right then, for a bull tag!

Recommitting to the hunt at hand, I eased my safety forward. The cow hadn't moved. Even with a perfectly still shot at a non-moving target, it was the longest shot I would even consider attempting. Three hundred yards in a fairly decent left-to-right wind. This was my opportunity, and it was now or never.

The thunder from my rifle caused every elk on the ridge to go from zero to sixty in 3.2 seconds. And my cow led the way! A clean miss.

Looking back at Rich, we both just kind of grinned at one another.

Oh, well.

REFLECT

If you could create the dream hunt of a lifetime, what would it be? Describe it in one very specific paragraph:

_____

_____

_____

_____

_____

_____

_____

_____

LOOK AT THE BOOK

King David went in, sat in the Lord's presence, and said, "Who am I, Lord God, and what is my house that You have brought me this far?"—2 Samuel 7:18

David was an interesting man to say the least—a man of incredible stamina who had the heart of a king and the heart of God. He was strong. And weak. Wise in battle, but not too smart with women.

In the end he was just a man.

When I read this verse of David's prayer, it births in me a sneaking suspicion that David never expected too much from himself. As strange as that may seem, I believe it's true. One of the greatest mistakes we make as believers is to grossly exaggerate the people of the Bible into these larger-than-life heroes.

Think about it for a minute: you believe Jesus was the Son of God, right? Yet I'll bet you have a really hard time imagining Jesus as a real man with real struggles. When a pretty girl walked by, do you think He wanted to turn His head? You bet He did. He was a man. So was David.

So when I read David's humility, when I hear him reflecting back on a life filled with a over-arching sense of God's blessing and provision, I sense him basically saying, "Why has all of this come to me? I don't get it really. Who am I to deserve this?"

It's a good question to ask ourselves.

DIG DEEPER

1. Just as there are seasons of the hunt, there are seasons of the soul. What spiritual season are you in right now?

_____

_____

_____

_____

_____

2. How different would your life be right now if you looked at your world the way God does?

_____

_____

_____

_____

_____

3. Write a prayer describing your desire to see the big picture of God's presence during this season of your life.

_____

_____

_____

_____

_____

_____

FROM THE HEART

My first trip into the high country was a complete success because I planned it that way from the beginning. I knew that my chances of taking a nice buck weren't that high. It wasn't a guided hunt on a professional outfitter's ranch. And that was the way I wanted it. There was no 85 percent success rate guaranteed in my package.

Sure, those types of hunts are great. Yet this was my first chance to hunt out west and I was literally thrilled just to get to go. I made up my mind ahead of time that the entire hunt would be a success. The flight out, the relationships made, the dinners, seeing new country for the first time, all of it.

As hunters I believe we can get so caught up in the size of the rack that we completely miss the trip. What kind of legacy does that pass down to our sons and daughters? Hunts that end with large racks are not the only successful ones. My hunt in Oregon was a success from the minute I got there. Just being there filled the tag in my soul. So I can ask along with David, "Who am I that You have brought me this far?"

POSTSCRIPT

The Lord had led David all the way—over the rocks, through the battles. All the way, love led him. That's what made him a success. And he knew it. We need to remember, too, that no matter what we do, it's a success if God is in it!

Acknowledgements from Jimmy Sites

Jason Cruise—Thank you for answering the call of the Lord and the call of the wild. You have merged these two passions well and are allowing God to use you in awesome ways. I count it a privilege to co-author this book with you.

Lawrence Kimbrough—Your patience with my schedule as well as your skills with my words should place you in the Boone and Crockett record book for "Best Editor of the Year." If there were such a category, you would score high.

TeamSOA—You are an amazing team of men and women who love the Lord even more than hunting or fishing. The journey over the past few years has been mind-boggling! Thanks to my Board of Directors, my crew in the field, and the faithful back at the SOA Log Lodge headquarters. Thanks to our sponsors who contribute to the ministry of spreading God's Word across the world in a very unconventional way, the outfitters who always go the second mile to make our trips successful, and our faithful television viewers and radio listeners. Without all of you, we would not be in existence as a ministry.

New River Fellowship—You are the most incredible church family I have ever experienced. Living life with you is like rafting a level five white water river. Thank you for your love, support, and encouragement. It is a privilege to serve as one of your pastors.

Mom and Dad—You are the guilty ones! You both placed within me a love for the outdoors. You also introduced me to Jesus Christ. You taught me to love Him and follow His trail, how to care for the poor and the disadvantaged, and how to live with a passionate desire to show lost people where salvation is. Thank you from the deepest part of my heart. I love you both!

Christin—My firstborn. I am in awe of the woman I see developing in you. Your heart is so amazing, and your commitment to the Lord God is far beyond the level of most teenagers. You are beautiful inside and out. I love you so much I would give up hunting and fishing for you if the need arose. Hopefully it won't.

Jonathan—You are the son every man dreams of. You're an incredible athlete and outdoorsman at a very young age. But if these things all went away, it wouldn't change how I feel about you. You are becoming a powerful young man of God. You embrace adventure, love deeply, live fully, and share selflessly. I am proud to call you my son.

Amanda—You have to carry a heavier load at home when I am hiking the high country of the world in pursuit of the next great adventure. When I'm home, you are so faithful in supporting the time I need to do what I do, including the writing of this book. I'm convinced that I married an angel. Words are not adequate to express how much I love and appreciate you. Thanks for being my number one partner in the adventure of life.

Acknowledgements from Jason Cruise

Jesus—Your Word tells me that you created the sod under my boots. Following You is the greatest adventure ever. Lead on, O King Eternal!

Michelle—Your support in reaching outdoorsmen for Christ means more than you'll ever know. And now we have our son to share it with. Can't wait to start seeing you in camo.

Larry Cruise—You bought me my first gun and my first bow. Took me fishing my first time. And captured my heart along the way. You are the best man I know.

Nancy Cruise—The greatest mom ever. You are the most Christlike person I know and my greatest cheerleader.

Jimmy Sites—For what you are doing in the outdoors and for all your contribution on this project. I look forward to watching what God does with you and SOA.

The ProStaff of Outdoor Ministry Network—You guys are the best team a guy could have. My heart is full.

Lawrence Kimbrough—I can't imagine God bringing me a finer friend. To have a publisher I trust deeply means more than I can fathom.

Rich Priday—For accompanying me on my first trip into the High Country. You're a great man who gave me great memories.

Hunters Everywhere—To all of you who have taken out your wallet and purchased this book. I pray it will guide you in the hunt that matters most . . . the hunt for a relationship with the God who made it all.

ALSO AVAILABLE
FOR HUNTERS AND OUTDOORSMEN

from Broadman & Holman Publishers

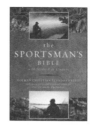

The Heart of
the Sportsman
0-8054-3094-6

The Sportsman's
Bible
1-58640-095-9

To book Jason Cruise for speaking engagements or to find help in how to establish outdoor ministry efforts in your church or community, contact him through www.outdoorministrynetwork.com

To contact Jimmy Sites about speaking engagements, to check on upcoming events, even to find a complete curriculum for use in reaching outdoorsmen for Christ—and much more—visit www.SpiritualOutdoorAdventures.org. In fact, many of the chapters from this book are paired with actual SOA episodes on DVD to make an effective teaching tool and outreach opportunity. Jimmy and his team can show you how.